IRIS HUTEGGER

CECI N'EST PAS UN PAYSAGE

Kunstmuseum Solothurn
Verlag für moderne Kunst, Wien

Inhalt — Contents

12 Vorwort und Dank —
13 Introduction and Thanks

14 **Heimatlos**
    Bilden und Auflösen in den Landschaften von Iris Hutegger
    CHRISTOPH VÖGELE

21 **Du fil dans les idées**
    Les photographies brodées d'Iris Hutegger
    KARINE TISSOT

28 **Rootless**
    Formation and Dissolution in the Landscapes of Iris Hutegger
    CHRISTOPH VÖGELE

34 **The Thread Running Through It**
    Iris Hutegger's Embroidered Photographs
    KARINE TISSOT

41 **Abbildungen — Pictures**

82 Liste der Abbildungen — List of Works
84 Iris Hutegger, Biografie und Ausstellungen — Biography and Exhibitions
86 Autoren — Authors
87 Impressum — Imprint

Vorwort und Dank

Diese Publikation erscheint zur Ausstellung *Iris Hutegger und Alice Bailly* im Kunstmuseum Solothurn. Damit wird das einzigartige Schaffen von Iris Hutegger (* 1964) erstmals mit einer grossen Museums-Präsentation gewürdigt. Während sich dieses Buch auf das Werk von Iris Hutegger konzentriert, ermöglicht die Ausstellung eine Begegnung zwischen den mit farbigen Fäden benähten Fotografien von Iris Hutegger und den Wollbildern der Schweizer Kubistin Alice Bailly (1872–1938). Mit Sophie Taeuber-Arp (1889–1943) gibt es eine zweite moderne Schweizer Künstlerin, welche die Stickerei als Ausdrucksmittel nutzte. Dass es sich bei beiden Kunstschaffenden um Frauen handelt, ist wenig erstaunlich – mehr noch die Tatsache, dass just das textile Handwerk zu einer stilistischen Radikalisierung beitrug: Während Sophie Taeuber-Arp gerade durch ihre Verbindung zur Ostschweizer Stickerei-Tradition und die Beschäftigung mit Textilmustern einen schnellen Weg zur konkreten Kunst fand, nutzte Alice Bailly die Einschränkung, die ihr der Wollfaden auferlegte, als Tugend. Abstraktion war nicht nur gefordert, sondern erwünscht. Und so können die figurativen Sujets ihrer dekorativ anmutenden *Tableaux-laine* oft erst auf den zweiten Blick erkannt werden.

Auch bei Iris Huteggers Fotografien dient die textile Ergänzung einem Prozess der Abstraktion und Distanzierung. Und doch können die textilen Schichten als «Verwirklichung» erlebt werden: Während die farbigen Fäden als Kolorierung der Schwarz-Weiss-Fotografie erscheinen, hebt sich die Stickerei als Geflecht von der Fläche ab. Wurde eine Angleichung von Kunst und Kunsthandwerk zu Zeiten des «Bauhauses» gesucht, bleibt die Verwendung von Textilien in der Kunst bis heute umstritten. Dies gilt zumal für «Landschaften», die vom selben Verdikt des Harmlosen betroffen sind wie Textilwerke aus Frauenhand. Gerade in ihrer ernsthaften «Unverblümtheit» aber liegt die Brisanz von Iris Huteggers Werken.

Unser Dank gilt zuallererst der Künstlerin Iris Hutegger, die sich mit grosser Sorgfalt für unser Projekt engagiert hat. Bemerkenswert ist die spontane Unterstützung, die uns ihre drei Galerien – Galerie Jacques Cerami, Charleroi; Galleria Martini & Ronchetti, Genua; Galerie Esther Woerdehoff, Paris – und verschiedene private Leihgeberinnen und Leihgeber gewährt haben. Auch den diversen Museen und Privatsammlungen, die uns ihre Werke von Alice Bailly anvertraut haben, gilt unser Dank. Zur Realisierung des im Verlag für moderne Kunst, Wien erscheinenden Buches haben viele Kräfte beigetragen: Wir danken Karine Tissot, Direktorin Centre d'art contemporain d'Yverdon-les-Bains, für ihren anregenden Aufsatz, Guido Widmer für die einfühlsame Gestaltung, Steve Gander und John O'Toole für die präzisen Übersetzungen sowie Serge Hasenböhler für die hervorragenden Fotografien. Für die finanzielle Unterstützung von Ausstellung und Buch richten wir unseren Dank an den Lotteriefonds des Kantons Solothurn, den Kanton Basel-Stadt sowie an die Schweizer Kulturstiftung Pro Helvetia. Last but not least danke ich meinem ganzen Team für den kompetenten Einsatz auf allen Ebenen.

Christoph Vögele

Introduction and Thanks

This publication accompanies the exhibition *Iris Hutegger und Alice Bailly* at Kunstmuseum Solothurn. The unique work of Iris Hutegger (* 1964) is thus being honoured for the first time with a large museum presentation. Whereas this book concentrates on Iris Hutegger's work, the exhibition stages an encounter between her photographs embroidered with coloured threads and the wool paintings by Alice Bailly (1872–1938) the Swiss Cubist. With Sophie Taeuber-Arp (1889–1943) there is a second modern Swiss artist who used embroidery as a means of expression. The fact that both of these artists are women is not so astonishing—more so the fact that it was precisely textile handwork that contributed to stylistic radicalisation: whereas Sophie Taeuber-Arp quickly found her way to concrete art on account of her connection to the east Swiss embroidery tradition and her interest in textile patterns, Alice Bailly made a virtue of the limitations imposed by the wool. Abstraction was not only demanded but also wanted. The figurative motifs of her decorative-looking *Tableaux-laine* can often only be seen at second glance.

With Iris Hutegger's photographs the addition of textiles serves a process of abstraction and distancing. And nevertheless the textile layers can be experienced as "realisation": while the threads appear as colouring of the black-and-white photography the embroidery lifts the braiding from the surface. Although a convergence of art and crafts was sought after at the time of Bauhaus, the use of textiles in art has remained controversial until today. This especially applies to "landscapes", which are labelled with the same verdict of harmless as textile works by women. However, the explosive power of Iris Hutegger's works lies precisely in their serious "bluntness".

Our thanks go first of all to the artist Iris Hutegger, who committed herself to our project with great care and attention. We should also mention the spontaneous support we have received from her three galleries—Galerie Jacques Cerami, Charleroi; Galleria Martini & Ronchetti, Genoa; Galerie Esther Woerdehoff, Paris—and several private lenders. We also thank the various museums and private collections who have entrusted us with their works by Alice Bailly. Many people have contributed to the creation of this book, published by Verlag für moderne Kunst, Vienna: we thank Karine Tissot, director of the Centre d'art contemporain d'Yverdon-les-Bains, for her stimulating essay, Guido Widmer for his empathetic design, Steve Gander and John O'Toole for their precise translations and Serge Hasenböhler for his excellent photographs. We give our thanks for the financial support for the exhibition and book to the Lottery Fund of the Canton of Solothurn, the Canton Basel-Stadt, and the Swiss Arts Council Pro Helvetia. And last but not least I would like to thank my whole team for their competent work at all levels.

Christoph Vögele

Heimatlos
Bilden und Auflösen in den Landschaften von Iris Hutegger

CHRISTOPH VÖGELE

Sind Geschichten Heimat, und ist Heimat das Wissen in dem Gefäss unseres Körpers? In diesem Behälter, der Erfahrungen sammelt und in dem alle Zeiten gleichzeitig sind?

Iris Hutegger über das Schaffen von Chiharu Shiota, 2004 [1]

Das Wesenhafte und Interessante von Iris Huteggers Schaffen liegt in seiner entschiedenen Unentschiedenheit, in seinem mit dem lateinischen «Inter Esse» gemeinten Dazwischen-Sein. Das Dabei-Sein und Teilnehmen, von dem die Etymologie des Wortes ebenfalls spricht, passt trefflich zur ungewöhnlichen Präsenz von Huteggers Werken, die die Aufmerksamkeit und Teilhabe des Publikums weckt – und es mit unvergesslichen Erlebnissen belohnt. Die Wahrnehmung steht im Zentrum: Durch die Vielfalt simultaner Wirkungen und Täuschungen wird das sinnliche Erfassen geschärft; Genuss und Irritation motivieren Hingabe wie Wachsamkeit. Bei solcher Komplexität, die hinter den bezaubernden, scheinbar harmlosen Landschaftsmotiven vorerst kaum vermutet wird, stellt sich immer neu die Frage: Was geschieht bei der Betrachtung dieser Landschaften? Was evozieren sie, und was sehen wir wirklich? Was denken und erinnern wir dabei – und warum? Damit sind nicht nur phänomenologische, sondern auch kulturelle, emotionale und existenzielle Aspekte angesprochen, welche die erstaunlich junge Bildgattung Landschaft ausmachen. Aus dem intensiven Betrachten ihrer berückend schönen, Konzentration wie Langsamkeit einfordernden Werke ergibt sich ein Nach-Denken, weil sich statt endlicher Klärung zunehmende Verwirrung einstellt über das, was wir eigentlich wahrnehmen. Dabei geht es um die alte philosophische Frage nach Bild und Wirklichkeit, Schein und Sein, auf die sich die bildende Kunst als modellhafte, illusionistische Parallel-Welt seit Jahrhunderten versteht. Dass Iris Hutegger solche Gedankengänge vertraut sind, zeigt sich nicht nur in ihrer Initiative für den 2011 gegründeten Basler Künstler-Treff «ArtPhilo» zum Thema Kunst und Philosophie, sondern auch in ihrem Hinweis auf die Bedeutung der Schriften von Vilém Flusser (1920–1991) und Jean Baudrillard (1929–2007), die sie vor einigen Jahren, in einer Phase der Neuorientierung,

in ihrem spezifischen Umgang mit der Fotografie bestärkt haben.

Schon die Frage, welchen Medien die Künstlerin verpflichtet ist, bleibt offen, verbinden sich doch im selben Einzelwerk Fotografie, Malerei, Zeichnung und Objektkunst so nahtlos, dass sich aus dem Disparaten ein neues Ganzes bildet, das unser Auge kaum mehr zu trennen vermag, zumal aus einer dem ganzen Bild und nicht dem Detail verpflichteten Distanz. Unsere Fähigkeit zur präzisen Wahrnehmung ist Iris Huteggers ungemein feinem Zusammenspiel von Auge und Hand oft weit unterlegen – und nur die Künstlerin allein kann noch die Ebenen der verschiedenen Medien zweifelsfrei unterscheiden. Dass sie damit unseren Glauben an das Bild zerstört – wie ihr eine Betrachterin einmal vorwarf –, ist ihr nicht nur genehm, sondern als erklärte Absicht hoch willkommen. Denn die Verunsicherung motiviert eine Schärfung der Sinne und dadurch ein intensiveres Erleben, bei dem der Fokus zunehmend vom Objekt zum Subjekt der Wahrnehmung wechselt: zum Betrachter selbst als einem offenen, körperhaften Wesen.

«Ich bin Bildhauerin»
Wenn Iris Hutegger einem eigenen, 2014 während eines Arbeitsaufenthalts in Island geschriebenen Text den Titel «Ich bin Bildhauerin»[2] gibt, mag sie auf die Bedeutung solch körperhafter Wahrnehmung ansprechen. Tatsächlich hatte sich Iris Hutegger, noch bevor sie ab 2001 an der Hochschule für Design und Kunst Luzern und ab 2002 an der Hochschule für Gestaltung und Kunst Basel eine mehrjährige künstlerische Ausbildung absolvierte, der Bildhauerei zugewendet. Im Zentrum stand damals der Mensch, der in ihren heutigen Landschaften als Bildmotiv auffallend fehlt. Schon in ihren zwischen 2003 und 2005 entstandenen Faden-Installationen, die ein vergleichbares Interesse für das Plastische

des Raumes spiegeln, war er als Motiv abwesend. Dabei wurde indes spürbar, dass der Mensch in anderer Weise durchaus präsent war. Das hat nicht nur mit dem allgemeinen Wesen von Installationen zu tun, die sich auf den vorhandenen Raum und den ihn betretenden, realen Menschen beziehen, sondern zuweilen auch mit Iris Huteggers spezifischer Wahl alltäglicher Sujets, die sie als blosse Fadenzeichnung dreidimensional umreisst. Bemerkenswert ist das Motiv des Stuhles, der sich trotz seiner abstrahierten und ephemeren Gestalt im Raum behauptete und einen möglichen Nutzer evozierte. In einem Interview mit Elena Monzo äusserte sich die Künstlerin zu den betreffenden Hintergründen: «Ich arbeitete an einer Installation über eine Person, die im Raum anwesend und doch abwesend sein sollte. Dafür wählte ich vorerst einen alten Stuhl, doch ich mochte ihn nicht. Alle hätten den Stuhl als spezifisches Beispiel einer bestimmten Zeit gesehen. Er sagte zu viel über sich selbst. In diesem Moment wurde mir klar, dass nur eine einfache Zeichnung den Stuhl gleichzeitig universell wie individuell zeigen konnte.»[3] Mit dem Bildhauer und Zeichner Alberto Giacometti (1901–1966) nennt Iris Hutegger ein Vorbild der Kunstgeschichte, in dessen Schaffen Präsenz und Absenz, Körper, Raum, Vorstellung und Erinnerung eng miteinander verbunden sind. Und in gewisser Weise reflektieren ihre Installationen nicht nur ihre intensive Auseinandersetzung mit der japanischen, ebenfalls mit Fäden arbeitenden Installations-Künstlerin Chiharu Shiota (* 1972)[4], sondern auch mit Giacomettis filigranen Zeichnungen, in denen Gegenstände und Körper mit hauchfeinen Linienbündeln suggeriert werden.

Auf den ersten Blick scheint der Weg von Iris Huteggers Installationen aus Fäden zu ihren mit farbigen Fäden bestickten Fotografien weit. Und doch vermittelt die «Zeichnung» in beiden Werkgruppen zwischen dem Betrachter und dem real existierenden Raum. Dies ist für die in den Ausstellungsraum gespannten Installationen offensichtlicher als für die mit Fäden «kolorierten» Fotografien. Aber auch hier verdichten sich die Fäden letztlich zu dreidimensionalen Gebilden, die wie Moose das felsige Terrain der fotografierten Orte bewachsen und so die schwarz-weisse Abstraktion verlebendigen. Während die tiefen Bildrahmen, welche die Landschaften fast wie in einem Guckkasten wahrnehmen lassen, den plastischen Charakter der Werke betonen, binden die Passepartouts, welche die Darstellungen wie Zeichnungen fassen, den Blick zurück auf die Zweidimensionalität eines Bildes. Dadurch ergibt sich die eingangs erwähnte Unentschiedenheit, nicht nur zwischen den Medien und Dimensionen, sondern auch zwischen materieller Tatsache und Vorstellung, zwischen aktueller Wahrnehmung und Erinnerung.

«Non finito» und Erfindung
Paradoxien machen in vielfacher Weise das Schaffen Iris Huteggers aus. Betrachten wir etwa ihre Landschaften aus der Nähe, fällt auf, dass die Fadenzeichnung, welche die Fotografien bedeckt, oft nicht nur farblich, sondern auch linear weit von unseren organischen und natürlichen Landschafts-Vorstellungen abweicht und sich notgedrungen, Stich um Stich, in abstrakter Weise verdichten muss. Wie bei ihren Installationen, in denen sich die Fäden netzartig im Raum verspannen, in geometrischen Winkeln sich kreuzen, kann die Künstlerin an der Nähmaschine nur in geometrisch regelhaftem «Staccato» zeichnen. Dies wird nicht überall sogleich sichtbar, am schnellsten bei einigen der spärlicher benähten Werke (z.B. Abb. S. 56 und S. 73), in denen die farbigen Nähte offensichtlich von den topografischen Linien abweichen, um ihre «eigenen Wege» zu gehen. Bei anderen Landschaften wiederum wird die Stickerin zur «Malerin», die in glaubhaften

Farbtönen zwischen Grün und Blau dem Schwung einer Bergkuppe präzis folgt und diese in zauberhaftem Licht- und Schattenspiel modelliert (Abb. S. 55). Überhaupt erinnern manche der Schwarz-Weiss-Abzüge mit ihren inselhaften Farbstellen an frühe Fotografien, die punktuell von Hand koloriert wurden. Solches «Non finito» regt in besonderem Masse unsere Fantasie an und ruft nach individueller Vollendung. Nur selten bedecken die Stickereien das ganze Format. Als Beispiel lässt sich eine in differenzierten Grüntönen gehaltene Nahansicht nennen, die ein von Felsen und Wildwuchs durchsetztes alpines Gelände zeigt (Abb. S. 76). Das Bild wirkt wie ein fein geknüpfter Teppich, der fast vergessen lässt, dass ihm eine Fotografie zugrunde liegt. Im Miteinander von schneller Fotografie und wochenlanger Benähung versöhnen sich die Extreme in paradoxer Weise.

Orientierung und Sehnsucht
So unterschiedlich Iris Huteggers Landschaften auch anmuten, so konstant ist unser Drang, sich in ihnen zu orientieren, zu verorten, als stünden wir leibhaftig in ihnen. Ein Urinstinkt, ein Überlebenstrieb? Da die ausgesuchten, vielfach mit Weglassungen oder Ergänzungen manipulierten Darstellungen keinerlei Hinweise auf reale Orte geben, wird diese primäre existenzielle Suche noch verstärkt. Wie verirrte Wanderer in einsamer Natur fragen wir: «Wo bin ich? Und wie finde ich meinen Weg?» Es ist merkwürdig, mit welchem Eifer wir selbst in den kühnsten Abstraktionen noch «unsere» Landschaft zu finden hoffen.

Die wechselnde Aufnahme, die ihre Werke beim Publikum unterschiedlicher Länder finden, hat Iris Huteggers Interesse für die Landschaft als kulturelle Prägung und individuelles Erinnerungs-Bild geweckt. Bei ihren Beobachtungen hat sie etwa festgestellt, dass «die Verweildauer bei vertrauten Bildern deutlich länger» ist. «Besteht ein Vorwissen der abgebildeten Landschaft, so reicht ein kleiner Anreiz von Farbe und Struktur in Verbindung zum S-W-Fotobild, um beim Betrachter eine Illusion der Realität auszulösen.»[5] Die vertrauten Landschaften werden uns tatsächlich zur Heimat und prägen auch die späteren topografischen Vorlieben. Diese entscheiden oft, ob wir uns an einem neuen Ort schnell oder nur langsam heimisch fühlen können.

Solche Recherchen reflektieren die Ernsthaftigkeit, aus der Iris Hutegger die Kunst als Mittel der Erkenntnis betrachtet. Wichtig ist ihr auch die Klärung von Begriffen: «Für mich sind Landschaft und Natur zwei gänzlich unterschiedliche Begriffe, wenn nicht sogar voneinander unabhängige Bezeichnungen. Ich glaube, dass der Blick auf die Landschaft erst möglich wurde, als sich eine Distanz zwischen Mensch und Natur schob.»[6] Tatsächlich gehört die Landschaft als eigenständige Ausdrucksform zu den jüngsten Bildgattungen der Malerei. Erst mit der Aufklärung gewinnt die Landschaft an Bedeutung, und mit der deutschen Romantik, später mit dem Impressionismus erlebt sie ihre Höhepunkte. Die zumeist in Städten lebenden Maler suchten die ländliche Umgebung als Gegenwelt, und das Malen in der Natur wurde zur selbstverständlichen künstlerischen Gepflogenheit. Nachdem die Landschaft über Jahrhunderte nur als Hintergrundmotiv genehm war, entwickelte sie sich im 19. Jahrhundert schnell zur Lieblingsgattung des Publikums – und ist es bis heute geblieben. Seit Denis Diderot wurde verschiedentlich auf den Zusammenhang zwischen der Beliebtheit gemalter Landschaften und der zunehmenden Naturferne ihrer Käufer hingewiesen. Dass die malerische Ausdrucksform der Idylle ihre Blüte just ab Mitte des 19. Jahrhunderts fand, als Industrie, Technik und Verstädterung voranschritten, ist sprechend.[7]

Distanzierung, Verfremdung, Verunsicherung
Die mit der Kunstgattung der Landschaft verbundenen Sehnsüchte, die das Publikum in die entsprechenden Ausstellungen zieht, werden von Iris Hutegger kritisch hinterfragt. Wenn sie als landschaftlichen Bezug vorerst den Alpenraum wählt, wendet sich die gebürtige Österreicherin vertrauter Topografie zu. Allerdings unternimmt sie bei der Bearbeitung ihrer Werke viel, um sich vom Gesehenen als Heimat zu distanzieren. Sprechend ist denn auch der Ursprung ihrer ganz eigenwilligen, ihr gleichsam zugefallenen Technik des Benähens von Fotografien: Verzweiflung und Wut haben sie nämlich eine ihrer Fotografien unter die Nähmaschine legen lassen – um dem schönen und ihr wohl falsch erscheinenden Erinnerungsbild zu Leibe zu rücken. Bereits um 2004/2005, gleichzeitig mit ihren Faden-Installationen, waren Schwarz-Weiss-Fotografien entstanden, die deutliche Kratzspuren aufwiesen. Dazu schreibt die Künstlerin: «Landschaften als Räume die nicht mehr *verortet* sind. Landschaften als Räume die nicht mehr *verjahreszeitet* sind. / Verletzungen der Oberfläche wie Einstiche, Kratzspuren schaffen ein neues Bild. / Verletzung und Gestaltung in Einem.»[8]

Die Verfremdung ihrer heutigen Landschaften beginnt schon damit, dass sie die ursprünglichen Farbaufnahmen auf einem Schwarz-Weiss-Fotopapier abzieht. Die unterschiedlichen Lichtwerte, die sich bei der klassischen Schwarz-Weiss-Fotografie in aller Schärfe und Differenzierung zeigen, scheinen nun malerisch ineinanderzufliessen. Zuweilen wirken die Aufnahmen wie weiche Kohle- oder Bleistiftzeichnungen. Bedient sich die Künstlerin zur Ergänzung ihrer Fotografien tatsächlich dieser Techniken, sind diese kaum oder gar nicht mehr vom eigentlichen Abzug zu unterscheiden. Eine weitere Form der bewussten Distanzierung erfolgt durch die lange Zeitspanne, die sie verstreichen lässt, bevor sie ihre Fotografien, die sie in Österreich und der Schweiz, in Griechenland, Island oder den Vereinigten Staaten gemacht hat, überarbeitet. Damit hofft sie auf das Vergessen der entsprechenden Erinnerungen. Denn nur so kann sie die Landschaften neu sehen und darum auch mit neuen Farben übernähen. Solch eigener, erfundener Palette geht also ein doppeltes Löschen natürlicher Farbigkeit voraus: zum einen durch den Abzug eines Farbbildes auf schwarz-weissem Fotopapier, zum anderen durch den Prozess des Vergessens.

Löschen und Überschreiben sind Gepflogenheiten des elektronischen Zeitalters. Und doch verwendet Iris Hutegger für ihre Landschaften mit Absicht alte Techniken: analoge Fotografie im klassischen Silbergelatine-Abzug, Zeichnung, Gouache und Stickerei. Wenn sie die analoge der digitalen Fotografie vorzieht, so entscheidet sie sich für die Freiheit, ihre Werkzeuge jederzeit beherrschen und für ihre künstlerischen Absichten einsetzen zu können. Der sinnliche und lebendige Ausdruck ihrer Werke bezieht sich gerade auf die in der Arbeit sichtbar werdende Zeit-Spur: Aus der Nähe können wir den einzelnen Stichen ihres Nähens ebenso klar folgen wie den sichtbaren Pinselzügen eines Gemäldes oder dem Linienverlauf einer Zeichnung.

Trompe-l'œil, Abstraktion und Wirklichkeit
Die alten Techniken führen gleichwohl nicht zurück zu einem herkömmlichen Landschaftsbild, auch wenn die Werke mit ihrer erstaunlichen Angleichung unterschiedlicher Medien die lange Tradition des Trompe-l'œil fortsetzen. Beispiele dieses Genres verblüffen nicht nur durch ihre stupende Technik; hinter der vordergründigen Virtuosität verbirgt sich zugleich philosophisches Denken: Die Entdeckung des Augentrugs lenkt den Blick vom Gezeigten ab und öffnet ihn für anderes. Und auch bei Iris Huteggers Werken verlieren die Motive im Verlaufe der Betrachtung immer mehr an Bedeutung.

Bei der zunehmenden Verwirrung, was mit dem scheinbar Gleichen – Landschaften, nichts als Landschaften – anzufangen sei, suchen wir nach formalen Gesetzmässigkeiten, ohne sie wirklich zu finden: Wie sind die Bilder komponiert? Wo befinden sich die Farbstellen? Wie wird Räumlichkeit suggeriert? Und wo ist der Platz des Betrachters? Die entsprechenden Antworten hängen oft mit Wirkungen und Stimmungen zusammen: Strahlend oder trüb, bedrohlich oder zauberhaft, finden die evozierten Gefühle vor allem über die Palette ihren Ausdruck. Bei längerer Betrachtung fällt auf, wie abstrakt viele der Landschaften anmuten: Da werden scharf geschnittene Bergsilhouetten unter das blanke Weiss eines Himmels gesetzt (Abb. S. 55, S. 56), blaue und violette Farbbänder in das Wogen sanfter Hügelzüge gelegt (Abb. S. 57). In einem Hochformat fliesst uns leuchtendes Rot entgegen, das seinen Weg durch ein Bett von Geröll findet und dabei weniger an das Blühen alpiner Flora als an einen Blutstrom denken lässt (Abb. S. 67). Dass sich selbst die unnatürlichsten Farben noch scheinbar stimmig ins illusionistische Gelände legen, hat verschiedene Gründe: Zum einen respektiert die Künstlerin beim Nähen die Horizontlinie und betont durch dichtere Stiche die Bergsilhouetten, zum anderen antwortet sie mit spezifischen Gestaltungsweisen auf vorhandene Strukturen. Dabei finden sich sowohl Angleichung wie bewusste Kontrastierung: Während sie hier in radikaler Weise mit einer bunten Palette von Orange, Weinrot, Hellblau und Violett die Bildgründe hemmungslos übernäht und damit einen plausiblen Ausdruck für den Wildwuchs mediterraner Macchie findet (Abb. S. 68), setzt sie dort mit farbigen Punkten den Kiesel-Grund einer kargen Oberfläche einfühlsam fort (Abb. S. 42). Zur erstaunlich glaubwürdigen Wirkung trägt auch die plastische Erscheinung der textilen Stellen bei, die körperhaft leuchtend hervortreten: Ihre stoffliche Qualität suggeriert Natürlichkeit, macht Lust, die weichen Formen zu berühren. Gerade weil wir diese farbigen Gespinste scheinbar greifen können, müssen wir sie wohl nicht mehr gedanklich begreifen und infrage stellen. So lehren uns Iris Huteggers Werke, zwischen Natürlichkeit und Wirklichkeit zu unterscheiden. Denn was auf uns wirkt, uns berührt und bewegt, muss nicht zwingend natürlich sein, auch wenn die Motive mit der Vorstellung des Natürlichen spielen. Ermöglicht wird ein reines Schauen, ein langsamer, fast hingebungsvoller Prozess der Vertiefung. Darin gleichen ihre landschaftlichen Abstraktionen den innigen Andachtsbildern der nordischen Spätgotik.

Die Landschaft als Bildgattung ermöglicht nicht nur eine farbliche Abstrahierung des Natürlichen, sondern auch eine grundsätzliche Befragung von Naturstimmungen als Spiegel universeller menschlicher Gefühle. Darin können Iris Huteggers Landschaften auf die Kunst der deutschen Romantik bezogen werden. Tatsächlich gibt es eine Reihe von Werken, die in ihrem melancholischen Ausdruck die romantische Tradition fortsetzen. Bemerkenswert sind mehrere, auffallend dunkeltonige Arbeiten: Während die Künstlerin eine kleinformatige Berglandschaft sehr dicht mit schwarzen und gelben Fäden bestickt, mit Bleistift den Himmel verdunkelt, als zöge demnächst ein schweres Gewitter auf (Abb. S. 71), bedeckt sie in einem anderen Werk den Himmel gänzlich mit schwarzer Farbe, um das darunter liegende Gelände umso greller erscheinen zu lassen. Mit den merkwürdigsten Farbtönen zwischen Violett, Hellblau und Orange trägt sie zu einer weiteren Verfremdung dieser fast apokalyptisch anmutenden Szene bei (Abb. S. 75).

Zauberhaft wirkt dagegen das Bild eines zwischen Hügeln und Steilwänden liegenden Bergsees (Abb. S. 45): Alles in dieser weitgehend unfarbigen Landschaft wirkt zeichnerisch weich, leicht und hell.

Und wo die Künstlerin einzelne Stellen der Fotografie noch zu hart fand, hat sie diese mit weissem Faden aufgehellt oder ausgelöscht. Der Zauber, der dieser silbern klingenden Landschaft eigen ist, verbindet sich einmal mehr mit der Ungewissheit über Tatsache und Wirkung: Sehe ich im grauen Weichbild tatsächlich Farben, oder stelle ich sie mir nur vor? Und können nicht auch die blossen Lichtwerte eines Schwarz-Weiss-Abzuges farbig wirken?

In-der-Welt-Sein: Landschaft als Existenz-Bild
Bei der Frage, was Iris Huteggers Landschaften von den Werken der deutschen Romantik unterscheidet und was innerhalb der Tradition existenzieller «Seelenbilder» ihren zeitgenössischen Beitrag ausmacht, kann nochmals auf das eingangs erwähnte «Inter Esse» verwiesen werden, das sich vom herkömmlichen Austausch zwischen Künstlerin, Kunstwerk und Betrachter unterscheidet. Das Dazwischen-Sein ist nämlich geprägt von allseitiger Kommunikation, bei der die Künstlerin nicht nur schöpferisch agiert, sondern ebenso oft reagiert, indem sie sich beim Nähen stetig mit etwas bereits Vorhandenem beschäftigen muss. Und der Betrachter ist nicht mehr nur ein passiver Betrachter, sondern – wie beim Erleben einer Installation – ein mit allen Sinnen wahrnehmender Teilhaber.

Sind Iris Huteggers Bilder überhaupt Landschaften? Ihre Titel nennen statt Motiven nur Zahlen: Die beiden ersten Ziffern stehen für das Jahr der Fertigstellung des betreffenden Werkes, die folgenden für den jeweiligen Monat; und bei den letzten, nachgestellten Ziffern handelt es sich um die jeweilige Werknummer. «Landschaft» ist vor allem ein kunsthistorischer Begriff, eine kulturelle Erfindung, die mehr über unser existenzielles In-der-Welt-Sein, unsere Weltanschauung sagt als über einen spezifischen Ort. Auch Iris Huteggers Landschaften zeigen keine Heimat im herkömmlichen Sinn, auch wenn die Künstlerin mit ihren Bildern just dort begonnen hatte, wo sie sich heimisch fühlte, in der Bergwelt ihrer (Wahl-)Heimat. Die Frage nach Geborgenheit ist trotzdem zentral. Denn die plastisch wirkenden, stark auf den Betrachter ausgerichteten Werke drehen sich letztlich um die grundlegende Frage von Raum und Verortung. Darin verbindet sie, wie ihr Vorbild Alberto Giacometti, die künstlerische Frage der Darstellbarkeit von Wirklichkeit mit der Suche nach einem aktuellen Bild menschlicher Existenz. Gerade im Zeitalter der Virtualität, die eine Orientierung zunehmend erschwert, will uns Iris Hutegger keine Illusionen machen. Gleichwohl widmet sie sich mit solcher Hingabe der Suggestion sinnlicher Wirklichkeit, dass wir ihre Landschaften wenigstens als Modellwelt landschaftlichen Erlebens auffassen können.

Der Körper als mögliche Heimat
Letztlich aber richtet sich ihr Blick weniger auf die Wahrnehmung von Welt, die zunehmend undurchschaubarer und trügerischer wird, als auf den Körper, der diese Welt dennoch mit allen Sinnen wahrnehmen möchte. Dafür sprechen nicht nur die Bedeutung des Handwerks als Realitätsbezug, sondern auch die haptische Präsenz und Wirkung des Schaffens, die den Betrachter in einen Zustand körperlicher Wachheit versetzt. Iris Hutegger hat den Körper bereits in einem Text über Chiharu Shiota als möglichen Ort von Heimat vermutet: Der Körper wird zum Speicher, in dem Geschichten, Erfahrungen und Erinnerungen lagern und sich verdichten, zum Behälter, «in dem alle Zeiten gleichzeitig sind»[9]. Dieselbe Beschreibung liesse sich auch auf die Bild-Körper ihrer Landschaften anwenden.

In vielfacher Hinsicht ist «Heimat» zur Mode, zum Schlagwort für Politik und Werbung geworden, in einer Zeit, in der ein spezifischer Heimatbezug zunehmend schwieriger, ja suspekter geworden ist.

Wenn Iris Hutegger Landschaften erfindet, die uns letztlich fremd bleiben, so antwortet sie auf ein zunehmendes Gefühl der Heimatlosigkeit. In ihren Werken aber spiegeln sich Werte, an denen sich Halt finden lässt: Arbeit als Erfüllung, Differenzierung als Reichtum, Sinnlichkeit als Lebenskraft.

1 Iris Hutegger, *Geschichten. Netzwerk, Betten Le_rstellen im Werk von Chiharu Shiota,* Vordiplom II, FHBB HGK Basel, Abt. Bildende Kunst/Medienkunst, unveröffentlichtes Typoskript, August 2004, S. 6.
2 Iris Hutegger, *Ich bin Bildhauerin,* unveröffentlichtes Typoskript, Oktober 2014.
3 Interview zwischen Elena Monzo, Mailand, und Iris Hutegger, Füllinsdorf, April 2015. Übersetzt nach einem englischen Typoskript, S. 6.
4 Vgl. Fussnote 1. – Iris Hutegger hatte 2002 in der Ausstellung *Another World – Zwölf Bettgeschichten* des Kunstmuseums Luzern eine Installation von Chiharu Shiota gesehen. Sie war so tief davon beeindruckt, dass sie dem Werk 2004 ihre Basler Vordiplomarbeit widmete. Im Unterschied zu Shiota, die für ihre Luzerner Installation 20 Betten verwendete, verzichtete Hutegger aber für ihre eigenen Faden-Installationen konsequent auf die Integration von Alltagsgegenständen.
5 Iris Hutegger, *Ich bin Bildhauerin,* wie Fussnote 2, S. 3.
6 Ebenda.
7 Vgl. Rolf Wedewer, Jens Christian Jensen (Hrsg.), *Die Idylle. Eine Bildform im Wandel. Zwischen Hoffnung und Wirklichkeit. 1750–1930,* Köln: DuMont, 1987. – Barbara Eschenburg, *Landschaft in der deutschen Malerei,* München: C.H. Beck, 1987 (hier vor allem das Kapitel «Industrialisierung und Naturverklärung», S. 165–181).
8 Heft «Fotografien 2004/2005» aus einem achtteiligen Dossier mit Werkgruppen der Jahre 2003–2005, Publikation der Künstlerin, 2005.
9 Vgl. Motto, Fussnote 1.

Du fil dans les idées[1]
Les photographies brodées d'Iris Hutegger

KARINE TISSOT

Comme le peintre presse les tubes de couleur sur sa palette pour obtenir le ton recherché, comme le sculpteur prélève des morceaux du matériau qu'il travaille pour donner corps à une forme, Iris Hutegger use de protocoles spécifiques qui en appellent tour à tour au déchirement et à l'assemblage via une pratique singulière qu'est la couture. La plasticienne d'origine autrichienne mène un travail qu'elle nomme photographie, dessin, peinture et parfois sculpture et qui lui fait rencontrer la machine à coudre. Le papier photographique comme support en est le révélateur. Elle l'envisage physiquement, dans sa résistance. Il faut qu'une histoire se fasse, qu'une temporalité s'installe, qu'une nouvelle image se crée grâce au fil.

Le fil d'Ariane dans tous ses états
Depuis l'imaginaire antique et mythologique jusqu'à notre époque contemporaine, la symbolique du fil n'a pas changé : à travers le lien vital, il cristallise l'orientation de la vie. Dans la mythologie grecque, le fil de la destinée était tissé à la quenouille par les trois Moires[2], divinités du destin : la naissance était symbolisée par la quenouille que maniait Clotho, le fil des événements était représenté par le fuseau que Lachésis enroulait, et la mort était symbolisée par les ciseaux qu'Atropos maniait. Ariane dévida quant à elle son fil pour que Thésée trouve la sortie du labyrinthe, et Pénélope s'ingéniait à faire, défaire, refaire continuellement sa tapisserie afin de suspendre le temps et son destin.

Se déconnecter en brodant, délaisser pour un temps le monde environnant, ses problèmes et ses réalités. Longtemps échappatoire des femmes tout en étant symbole d'éducation pour des jeunes filles qui, au travers de leur trousseau, se tissaient un destin de futures femmes à marier, le travail du fil contient en son cœur un monde silencieux de narration, de tension et de sublimation qui prend différentes formes selon les époques et les cultures. Ayant pendant des siècles servi exclusivement à la couture ou à la broderie, le fil est dans le champ de l'art contemporain plus ou moins redevable à cette histoire-là, tour à tour figuratif ou abstrait, mais assurément gourmand d'idées : il permet de dire, d'exprimer, de travailler l'image bien au-delà de la tradition domestique, fonctionnelle ou décorative. Mixant les médiums pour mieux « abattre les murs » de cette dernière, le travail d'Iris Hutegger se situe assurément dans cette idée d'ouverture. L'espace de réalisation est méditatif et le temps un élément créateur.

De nos jours, force est de constater que les gestes de tissage ou de tressage ne relèvent plus *stricto sensu* du savoir-faire d'antan mais sont ritualisés pour faire naître des créations d'un autre ordre. Comme les monumentaux réseaux de fils de Chiharu Shiota[3] ou les lourds assemblages de fibres colorées déployés par Sheila Hicks[4]. C'est aussi en arachnéen que l'Argentin Tomás Saraceno[5] illustre ses théories des nuages ou que le Mexicain Gabriel Dawe[6] tisse des compositions colorées. Plus minimal, Fred Sandback[7] a laissé un œuvre conceptuel fait de quelques lignes poussant à son paroxysme la stratégie d'enlèvement de la matière dans la sculpture pour en éprouver au mieux la matérialité. Iris Hutegger marche en quelque sorte sur ses traces quand elle expérimente le dessin spatial dans les installations suivantes : *Freier Eintritt an allen Tagen* en 2009, *Doors and Stairs* en 2010 ou *Auch, Noch* en 2011[8].

Dans un autre genre, fils et filets s'entremêlent dans les travaux bricolés d'Annette Messager[9] qui explique qu'elle s'est « toujours intéressée aux arts dévalués. En tant que femme, [elle] étai[t] déjà une artiste dévaluée. Faisant partie d'une minorité, [elle est] attirée par les valeurs et les objets dits mineurs. De là sans doute, vient [son] goût pour l'art populaire, les proverbes, l'art brut, les sentences, les contes de fées, l'art du quotidien, les broderies, le cinéma[10] ».

Enfin, parallèlement au champ de l'art contemporain, depuis une dizaine d'années, le *yarn bombing*, autrement dit le *knit graffiti*, a pris ses quartiers sur la voie publique pour humaniser le tissu urbain, colorer le bitume et faire d'un art dit mineur – le tricot, le crochet, la couture – une force collective, souvent anonyme, dans nos sociétés individualistes. Ce tricot urbain pourrait être compris comme le pendant populaire des travaux baroques de l'artiste Joana Vasconcelos[11] mêlant tissus, vêtements et napperons aux broderies d'une extravagante complication, ou comme celui des tableaux de laine de Rosemarie Trockel[12] ou des pièces textiles d'Anni Albers[13] qui a su allier abstraction géométrique et pratiques vernaculaires liées aux cultures extra-occidentales.

Le fil appliqué

Quand le fil adhère fortement au support, tel que le pratique Iris Hutegger dans ses photographies, il peut prendre différents visages. Il se fait par exemple dessin dans les portraits de Sandrine Pelletier[14], cicatrice dans ceux d'Annegret Soltau[15], greffe chez Cathryn Boch[16] ou couleur dans les compositions hyperréalistes de Cayce Zavaglia[17]. En d'autres moments, il devient illustration dans le trait mi-encre mi-coton tracé conjointement par Isabelle Pralong[18] et Aurélie William Levaux[19] ou ornement dans les photographies des années 1950 rehaussées par Hinke Schreuders[20]. De même, il sait aussi bien jouer de souplesse dans un flottement lâche, comme en use abondamment Aglaia Haritz[21] ou comme en usait Maria Lai[22] dans ses écritures illisibles mais pas moins évocatrices d'états d'âme et de pensées. Au contraire il peut faire preuve de tension dans les masques de ficelles crochetés avec fermeté par Martine Birobent[23] pour museler et habiller des poupées ou dans le travail de « momification » d'objets mené par Alice Anderson[24] au moyen de fils de cuivre. Quant aux œuvres abstraites de Pierrette Bloch[25], elles insèrent le faireféminin retrouvant des mémoires enfouies par l'utilisation du fil sous des formes variées.

Qu'à cela ne tienne, le fil n'est plus seulement une affaire de femmes aujourd'hui, les *Mappa*[26], planisphères brodées initiées en 1971 et poursuivies jusqu'à la mort d'Alighiero e Boetti[27], comptent parmi les œuvres les plus célèbres de l'artiste issu de l'Arte Povera. Quant à Michael Raedecker[28], il situe la broderie au cœur de son travail, en ayant recours à des points très libres structurant la surface de ses peintures pour jouer d'effet de coulures et de touches.

« De fil en photographie[29] »

À l'instar de ce dernier – après avoir préalablement développé des expériences tridimensionnelles[30] comme mentionné plus haut – Iris Hutegger se sert désormais d'un premier médium – la photographie – pour y apposer un fil. L'introduction de la technique cousue – sans revendication délibérément féministe ni connotation féminine – y est discrète, ténue, comme une fine coquetterie. L'artiste exige du regardeur attention, curiosité et concentration s'il ne veut pas passer à côté du travail. C'est donc en s'approchant, en prenant le temps, en s'arrêtant vraiment, que l'on découvre le menu relief du fil, ses douces harmonies colorées[31] qui tranchent habilement avec les fonds paysagers noir et blanc.

Traces d'un « passage moiré » ou revêtement de végétation, difficile d'identifier ces rehauts de couleurs. On croirait par endroits reconnaître d'improbables coussins vert tendre de *Scleranthus uniflorus* sur les auges photographiées. Ce genre de mousse que l'on s'acharne à supprimer en Europe, alors qu'elle a une place de choix au pays du Soleil Levant : les jardins Saiho-ji, ou Kokedera – qui signifie par ailleurs « temple des mousses » – en contiennent plus de cent vingt espèces différentes. Cette diversité pourrait expliquer les variations allant du rouge au vert et tirant peut-être même parfois sur le vert-bleu dans les compositions d'Iris Hutegger. Quoi qu'il en soit, les mélanges de fils colorés n'aident en rien à l'identification des paysages qui, ramenés indifféremment d'Islande, des États-Unis, d'Autriche, de Suisse ou d'ailleurs risquent de prendre des airs immanquablement autres, simplement par le détournement des teintes originales.

Des vues de l'esprit
Bien que familière des montagnes autrichiennes et des Alpes helvétiques[32], Iris Hutegger « ne révèle jamais les lieux de [s]es photographies ». À travers le filtre du noir et blanc, la prise de vue traite uniformément la rudesse des falaises ou la douceur des courbes vallonnées, les surfaces d'eau et les roches au milieu des vallées, des prairies ou des forêts, se réclamant moins des forces subjectives et animées de l'art romantique que des vues de l'esprit. La couture épouse avec vigueur les formes photographiées tirées en noir et blanc quand bien même elles ont été captées en couleurs. Effet technique qui amenuise *de facto* les contrastes, saupoudrant les paysages d'un doux voile de camaïeu gris.

Sur ces grisailles, horizons évanescents, le fil dessine des traits nerveux, insistants, fournis. Il s'accroche à la pierre, à la terre mais ne s'étend jamais ni au ciel ni aux plans d'eau. Sous la pression de l'aiguille, le papier souffre et lâche timidement par endroits. Les lignes envahissent la surface de fils qui se tissent en profondeur, la matière se répartissant indifféremment devant et derrière la photographie. De cette manière, la couture insiste sur un jeu de visible et de caché, de présence et d'absence, d'apparition et de disparition par ce fil qui ravive l'idée de la couleur et dans le même temps n'est voyant que sur le recto. Un travail singulier qui émet des doutes sur la compacité du réel et sur l'ordre immuable des choses par un jeu subtil de lignes agitées, griffées. Comme une petite incertitude. Comme une délicate agitation. Une part du paysage est rongée insidieusement, le solide grignoté de part en part par des fils.

C'est peut-être par ce biais-ci que les compositions métissées d'Iris Hutegger invitent à la contemplation dans un moment en suspension. Le choix d'une palette restreinte, limitée à quelques teintes toujours dominées par le noir et blanc du fond, y contribue également. Permettant de révéler, comme dans la peinture traditionnelle chinoise, la richesse infinie d'un assortiment de couleurs : dans les photographies d'Iris Hutegger, comme dans les paysages chinois d'antan, pas besoin en effet de dire la couleur en couleurs. Là où l'encre de Chine plus ou moins épaisse permettait d'évoquer le monde, le travail d'Iris Hutegger offre une représentation mentale et universelle du paysage, sans s'attarder sur les détails de la nature représentée. Jamais aucune couleur ni aucun cadrage ne révèlent l'anecdotique – pas une fleur, pas un brin d'herbe –, bien au contraire, l'artiste tisse des lignes ou des aplats plus ou moins distincts les uns des autres, qui résonnent avec une idée de l'abstraction, esquivant la similarité avec la réalité de la prise de vue : « Quand je couds sur une photographie, je ne couds jamais d'herbe, de lichen ou de fleurs. Je travaille des structures, de la matière, des lignes qui peuvent déclencher des souvenirs. La couture pour moi a un haut degré d'abstraction. » En cela les vues choisies sont délibérément non-spectaculaires, s'ouvrant à un large champ d'interprétations possibles.

Prendre de la distance
Comme cela se pratiquait également dans l'Empire du Milieu, Iris Hutegger veille à prendre une distance avec son motif. Oublier le savoir pour retrouver un élan créateur. La comparaison avec la culture de l'autre continent permet d'insister sur des concepts comme l'inspiration ou le rythme, paramètres cardinaux d'une approche intuitive qui écarte toute analyse risquant d'enfermer le travail dans un discours. En poursuivant ce rapprochement avec la Chine traditionnelle, on pourrait comparer la *photographie* d'Iris Hutegger avec le *pinceau chinois* – qui tous deux produisent les formes, la structure, les grandes lignes – et le *fil* avec *l'encre* – qui ajoutent quant à eux les « rides », les modulations, les ombres et la lumière dans les compositions. Des composantes indissociables les unes des autres, comme le sont la chair et les os ou les montagnes et les lacs.

En définitive, Iris Hutegger applique au travers de son œuvre un thème récurrent : à travers des paysages plus ou moins grands, elle maintient ses vues à mi-chemin entre l'anonymat et l' « individualité ». Elle qui ne peut plus désormais séparer la photographie du fil insiste sur le fait que « le travail ne doit être qu'un ». Et de poursuivre : « Je m'intéresse au paysage en général », photographiant dans la permanence une idée du monde. « Le paysage est pour moi plus un espace mental. Il n'est constitué ni d'un début ni d'une fin, il est tout simplement cadré par l'image que l'on en fait à un moment donné. » Elle s'appuie sur la nature afin de retrouver la force créatrice du monde pour capter « l'insaisissable », une fois encore, si cher aux Chinois, ou peut-être même « la puissance de l'esprit de la vie ».

Un acte de destruction
Puis on pense au papier, surface que l'aiguille de la machine à coudre est venue transpercer. En regardant de près, on est partagé entre l'appréciation du travail raffiné et la perception presque tactile de l'idée de cicatrice, de balafre qui parcourt la photographie. Sensation que viennent renforcer de petits trous réalisés dans le papier et laissés plus ou moins grands. Car si la couture, comme la peinture, est une texture de travail, elle a toutefois la particularité de travailler aussi bien le dessus du support que l'arrière et l'entre-deux. La couture fige et désolidarise le papier en même temps. Elle reconstitue une matière autonome, contraint le support, lui donne du volume. L'aiguille utilisée par Iris Hutegger est mécanique, bruyante, elle ne glisse pas sur un tissu, n'assemble aucune pièce, mais malmène le papier photographique et l'ajoure par endroits. Au « fil » des virages, des accélérations, des retours, elle marque la feuille d'une trame serrée à l'extrême. Le papier accuse et garde cette empreinte de fibre dans la fibre. Il y a une forme de violence imposée au support, un risque pris à l'égard de l'image préexistante qui est amenée à être modifiée. Avec la machine à coudre, la tension est permanente, au sens propre comme au figuré. Ce qui explique l'utilisation d'un fil synthétique, plus résistant que le coton qui cède facilement dans ce genre d'usage[33].

Rappelons que dans l'œuvre d'Iris Hutegger, cette pratique de « photographie brodée » est née d'un premier acte de destruction : déçue par sa production photographique d'alors, Iris Hutegger s'énerve un jour – du temps de ses études – au point de la réduire à néant. Avant de s'en débarrasser, « apercevant la machine à coudre, [elle s']en [est] saisie aussitôt, sans arrière-plan ni réflexion pour tout détruire ». Une fois ses nerfs soulagés, l'artiste se surprend à observer le résultat : l'accident a révélé une texture insoupçonnée offrant la possibilité d'un nouvel essor à sa pratique photographique – « ce que l'aiguille a détruit a été recréé par le fil dans le même temps ». Désormais le fil permet aussi bien de tisser des toiles pour jouer de transparences par endroits que de recouvrir entièrement d'autres morceaux quitte à modifier l'image entière ou en partie. Pour Iris Hutegger, « le facteur le plus important dans cette manipulation réside précisément dans le fait que la photographie passe au statut d'image. Au travers de ce procédé, la photographie se marie avec l'idée du dessin – par le trait – de la peinture – par la couleur – et de la sculpture – par l'ajout de matière ». L'acte violent sera dès lors délibérément maîtrisé et contenu dans une forme d'esthétisme évitant toute surenchère ostentatoire qui aurait pu se traduire par des rapiècements, des gravures, des greffes ou des patchworks.

Éloge du silence et de la lenteur
Après les bruyants passages de la machine, le silence s'installe à nouveau dans l'atelier de l'artiste. Car c'est déjà en silence que les photographies d'Iris Hutegger ont été préalablement développées dans la chambre noire : « il me serait impossible de travailler la photographie digitale », précise-t-elle, bien consciente que son travail résonnerait différemment à feu l'ère de l'analogique. Le résultat de ses compositions contribue également à procurer une quiétude silencieuse au regardeur : « Le paysage dont je rends compte à travers mes photographies est toujours immaculé, sans chemin ni aucun autre signe de civilisation. » Il s'agit de montagnes, mais plus encore de minéraux et de végétaux qui, par leur immobilisme, dressent pour ainsi dire le décor des propos de Paul Virilio : « Depuis très longtemps, [...] je me revendique comme "terrien", et j'explique que nous devrions remplacer le terme "humain" par "terrien". Cela se justifie d'autant mieux quand on réalise que le terme "humain" vient de "humus", autrement dit de la terre. Je pense qu'au moment où nous perdons notre rapport à la terre, où l'on réduit le monde à rien par la vitesse, par le progrès, par l'accélération, il serait temps de nous reconnaître comme terriens. Nous faisons partie de l'espèce animale, nous sommes des êtres animés. C'est-à-dire qu'on se déplace, contrairement aux végétaux ou surtout aux minéraux[34]. »

À rebours d'un temps qui se consomme de nos jours à la hâte, Iris Hutegger conjugue plusieurs temporalités en une image qu'elle structure en profondeur. Des sommets millénaires captés en quelques fractions de seconde par l'appareil photographique, de l'image en couleurs ralentie par le procédé de développement au passage éclair d'une machine à coudre précise et déterminée, en passant par le choix de la couleur à broder qui peut parfois prendre des mois, le temps se conjugue au passé comme au présent : « Chaque trait est habité de sa propre histoire, dont il est l'expérience présente ; il n'explique pas, il est l'événement de sa propre matérialisation[35] », pour reprendre les termes de Cy Twombly. Enfin, le temps linéaire se lit symboliquement par le fil qui se dévide au gré de sa création et qui nous emmène vers notre fin selon les préceptes mythologiques.

À l'instar des femmes qui brodent, Iris Hutegger est focalisée sur son ouvrage, concentrée sur cette activité qui à la fois occupe l'esprit et le libère des turbulences de la pensée. Mais l'exercice de la plasticienne est bien loin de l'activité manuelle déstressante qui accapare l'attention. Plusieurs photographies sont travaillées dans le même temps, ceci permettant d'avancer de manière stimulante les compositions respectives menées parallèlement. Le travail sur l'une profite à l'autre et vice versa. L'ouvrage est remis sur le métier « au fil des idées ». Chaque composition préconise ses propres règles : « pas de couleur verte », « que du vert », « suivre la forme des Alpes », etc. Une manière d'éviter de diluer les intentions et de permettre de se concentrer sur un projet précis.

Le travail donne du « fil » à retordre. Par moment, il ne tient qu'à un « fil ». Certains travaux se situent sur le « fil » du rasoir : si le résultat ne convient pas, il sera complètement détruit.

« Perdre le fil »
Construit sur l'identité du geste, le travail d'Iris Hutegger questionne indéniablement l'héritage et les influences du répertoire ornemental de la « maison », que ce soit consciemment ou inconsciemment. Puisque le fait d'ajouter au moyen de l'aiguille, sur un fond préexistant, une ornementation de quelque nature qu'elle soit relève de la définition même de la broderie, utilisée depuis des âges. Mais son travail interroge essentiellement un art contemporain à la jointure du beau et de l'utile, mixant les codes de l'art, du design et de l'industrie. Rappelant que depuis des décennies, des liens viscéraux se tissent entre les mondes de l'art et du textile, dans l'effervescence de la modernité. En s'emparant du tissu et du fil certains artistes ont considérablement fait évoluer la notion de création dans la couture et inversement. De même les travaux oubliés des arts appliqués, qui n'ont jamais passé pour des œuvres d'art, ont retrouvé une grande force expressive et contemporaine depuis le siècle dernier. C'est sur cette voie-là que s'inscrit le travail d'Iris Hutegger, avec la volonté de donner à voir le même apaisement qu'apporte la contemplation d'un vrai paysage. Grâce à des fils qui, en ligne ou en épaisseur, lui permettent d'élaborer des mondes à part, inédits et improbables et tout à la fois si familiers et incertains. L'occasion enfin de rappeler que, contre les prétentions à la maîtrise, les incertitudes nous disent en effet que l'art consiste parfois à « perdre le fil » – celui d'Ariane, qui donne sens au labyrinthe comme à la vie –, et que le véritable labyrinthe n'est pas celui que construit Dédale mais celui auquel nous confronte l'image.

1. « Du fil dans les idées » est également le titre d'une exposition qui s'est tenue au Théâtre de la Tournelle à Orbe, du 7 au 29 novembre 2015, montée par le Centre d'art contemporain d'Yverdon-les-Bains, curatée par Karine Tissot. Les artistes suivants y étaient exposés : Martine Birobent, Joëlle Flumet, Liliana Gassiot, Aglaia Haritz, Stefanie Holler, Iris Hutegger, Aurélie William Levaux, Sandrine Pelletier, Isabelle Pralong, Sophie Schmidt et Garance Tschumi.
2. Nommées Moires (*moïra*, le destin, la fatalité) chez les Grecs et Parques (*pario*, enfanter, faire naître) chez les Romains.
3. Chiharu Shiota est née en 1972 au Japon, elle vit et travaille depuis 1996 à Berlin. Elle représentait le Japon à la Biennale d'art contemporain de Venise en 2015 avec une intervention de fils tendus dans l'espace selon des dimensions variables.
4. Sheila Hicks est née en 1934 aux États-Unis, elle vit et travaille à Paris depuis 1964. En 2014, elle exposait ses assemblages au Palais de Tokyo à Paris.
5. Tomás Saraceno est né en 1973 en Argentine, où il vit et travaille.
6. Gabriel Dawe est né en 1973 à Mexico, il vit et travaille à Dallas.
7. Fred Sandback (1943–2003), artiste américain.
8. *Freier Eintritt an allen Tagen*, 2009, a été réalisée dans l'exposition « Landscapes », Studio Rondo, Graz, Autriche ; *Doors and Stairs*, 2010, dans l'exposition « Bitte, Nehmen Sie Platz ! », artforum Spitzbart, Allemagne, et *Auch, Noch*, 2011, dans l'exposition « Regio Art Skulptur », Rehmann Museum, Laufenburg, Suisse. Toutes sont des installations où le fil d'Iris Hutegger s'est fait dessin dans l'espace.
9. Annette Messager est née en 1943 à Berck-sur-Mer, en France, elle vit et travaille en région parisienne.
10. Mercadé, Bernard, 2007, « L'artiste et ses doubles », *Beaux-Arts hors série « Annette Messager »*, 2007, 9, pp. 8–13
11. Joana Vasconcelos est née en 1971 à Paris, elle vit et travaille à Lisbonne.
12. Rosemarie Trockel est née en 1952 en Allemagne, où elle vit et travaille.
13. Anni Albers (1899–1994), artiste américaine d'origine allemande.
14. Sandrine Pelletier est née en 1976 à Lausanne, elle vit et travaille à Genève et à Bruxelles.
15. Annegret Soltau est née en 1946 en Allemagne, elle vit et travaille à Darmstadt.
16. Cathryn Boch est née en 1968 à Strasbourg, elle vit et travaille à Marseille.
17. Cayce Zavaglia est née en 1971 aux États-Unis, où elle vit et travaille.
18. Isabelle Pralong est née en 1967 à Sion, elle vit et travaille à Genève. Voir note suivante.
19. Aurélie William Levaux est née en 1981 en Belgique, où elle vit et travaille. Avec Isabelle Pralong, elle publie *Prédictions* aux Éditions Atrabile en 2011, illustrant sur des tissus avec stylo et aiguille des moments de la pièce de théâtre éponyme de Peter Handke.
20. Hinke Schreuders est née en 1969 aux Pays-Bas, où elle vit et travaille.
21. Aglaia Haritz est née en 1978 au Tessin, où elle vit et travaille. Depuis quelques années, elle a développé un projet itinérant dans le monde arabe avec l'artiste marocain Abdelaziz Zerrou autour de la condition de la femme dans ces régions, intitulé « Brodeuses d'actualité ».
22. Maria Lai (1919–2013), artiste italienne
23. Martine Birobent (1955–2016), artiste québécoise
24. Alice Anderson est née en 1976 à Londres, où elle vit et travaille.
25. Pierrette Bloch est née en 1928 à Paris, où elle vit et travaille.
26. « Des concentrés de temps », puisqu'elles ont parfois demandé jusqu'à cinq années de travail, réalisées par des tisserands ou des brodeuses d'Afghanistan, l'artiste étant rompu à la pratique de la sous-traitance.
27. Alighiero e Boetti (1940–1994), artiste italien
28. Michael Raedecker est né en 1963 à Amsterdam, il vit et travaille à Londres.
29. S'inspire de l'expression française « De fil en aiguille ».
30. Voir note 8
31. Iris Hutegger procède parfois à des rehauts de gouache ou de crayon en plus de la broderie.
32. Iris Hutegger a grandi en Autriche, au milieu des Alpes. Quand elle arrive en Suisse, elle s'établit d'abord dans le canton des Grisons, puis dans celui de Lucerne, deux régions entourées de montagnes. Aujourd'hui, établie à Bâle, elle vit à une heure de train des montagnes, ce qui lui offre par ailleurs une forme de distance par rapport au motif.
33. À noter qu'Iris Hutegger utilise toutefois du coton pour le noir, car la couleur est autrement plus dense.
34. *Culture mobile, penser la société du numérique*, « Paul Virilio, Terra Nova », entretien réalisé par Yvon Le Mignan et Ariel Kyrou le 17 novembre 2008.
35. Cité par Jean-Luc Nancy dans *Le Plaisir au dessin*, Paris, Éditions Galilé 2009, p. 54.

Rootless
Formation and Dissolution in the Landscapes of Iris Hutegger

CHRISTOPH VÖGELE

Are stories homeland, and is homeland the knowledge in the vessel of our body? In this container that gathers experience and in which all times exist simultaneously?

Iris Hutegger on the work of Chiharu Shiota, 2004[1]

The essential and interesting thing about Iris Hutegger's work is its decisive indecisiveness, its being in between, as expressed by the Latin "inter esse". Being there and participating, as also indicated by the etymology of the word, is very apposite for the unusual presence of Hutegger's works, which attract the attention and participation of the public—and reward it with unforgettable experiences. Perception is the central point: sensuous understanding is sharpened by the variety of simultaneous impressions and illusions: enjoyment and irritation motivate attention and alertness. With such complexity that would at first hardly be imagined behind these enchanting, apparently harmless landscape motifs, the question continuously arises: what happens when looking at these landscapes? What do they evoke and what do we really see? What do we think and remember—and why? It is thus not only phenomenological, but also cultural, emotional and existential aspects that go to make up the astonishingly new genre of landscape that are addressed. Intensive viewing of these enchantingly beautiful works, which call for concentration and slowness, results in re-flection because instead of ultimate clarification, increasing confusion arises as to what we actually perceive. It goes back to the old philosophical question of image and reality, appearance and being, in which for centuries the visual arts have seen themselves as an exemplary, illusionistic parallel world. The fact that Iris Hutegger is familiar with these lines of thought is shown not only by her initiative for the "ArtPhilo" artists' meetings on the subject of art and philosophy set up in Basel in 2011 but also by her reference to the importance of the writings of Vilém Flusser (1920–1991) and Jean Baudrillard (1929–2007), which reinforced her specific way of dealing with photography during a phase of reorientation several years ago.

Even the question of what media the artist is committed to remains open-ended. In the same individual work photography, painting, drawing and object art are combined so seamlessly that these disparate elements form a new whole that our eyes can hardly separate, especially when viewing from a distance to see the whole picture and not the detail. Our faculty for precise perception is often far inferior to Iris Hutegger's extraordinarily fine interplay of eye and hand—and only the artist can still distinguish with certainty the levels of the various media. The fact that she thereby destroys our belief in the picture—as a viewer once accused her—is not only agreeable to her but highly welcome as a declared aim. The uncertainty motivates a sharpening of the senses creating a more intensive experience, with the focus increasingly moving from the object to the subject of perception: to viewers themselves as open corporeal beings.

"I am a sculptor"

When Iris Hutegger entitles her text, written in 2014 during a working stay in Iceland, "Ich bin Bildhauerin"[2] ("I am a sculptor"), she may be alluding to the significance of such corporeal perception. In fact Iris Hutegger had turned to sculpture even before studying art for several years at the Hochschule für Design und Kunst Luzern from 2001 and from 2002 at the Hochschule für Gestaltung und Kunst Basel. At that time the central element was the human figure, which is noticeably absent as a motif in her current landscapes—as it is too in her thread installations, created between 2003 and 2005, which already reflected a comparable interest in the plasticity of space. Amongst all this, however, it could be felt that the human figure certainly was present in a different way. This not only has to do with the general nature of installations which relate to the available space and the real people who enter it but sometimes also with Iris Hutegger's specific choice of everyday subjects which she sketched three-dimensionally as pure thread drawings. The motif of the stool is notable; despite its abstracted and ephemeral form it asserted itself in the space and evoked a possible user. The artist discussed the background in an interview with Elena Monzo: "I was working on an installation about a person who was supposed to be present and nevertheless absent. At first I chose an old stool but I didn't like it. Everybody saw the stool as a specific example of a certain time. It was saying too much about itself. That's when it became clear to me that only a simple drawing could show the stool as both universal and individual at the same time."[3] As a model from art history Iris Hutegger names the sculptor and draughtsman Alberto Giacometti (1901–1966) in whose work presence and absence, body, space, imagination and memory are closely connected. And in a certain way her installations do not only reflect her intensive interest in the Japanese installation artist Chiharu Shiota (* 1972)[4], who also works with thread, but also in Giacometti's filigree drawings in which objects and figures are suggested by extremely fine clusters of lines.

At first glance it seems a long way from Iris Hutegger's thread installations to her photographs embroidered with coloured threads. But in both groups of works the "drawing" mediates between the viewer and the real existent space. This is more obvious with the installations spanned in the exhibition space than with the photographs "coloured" with threads. But here too the threads ultimately compact into three-dimensional images that grow on the rocky terrain of the photographed locations like moss and bring the black-and-white abstraction to life. The deep picture frames make the landscapes almost appear as if in a peep box and emphasise the plastic character of the work, while the passe-partouts frame the works like drawings and bring the eye back to the two-dimensionality of the pictures. This results in the previously mentioned indecisiveness, not only between the media and dimensions but also between material fact and imagination, between actual perception and memory.

"Non finito" and invention

Paradoxes sum up Iris Hutegger's work in many ways. If we take a close-up look at her landscapes, for example, it is noticeable that the thread drawing that covers the photographs is widely divergent from our organic and natural ideas of landscape, not only in terms of colour but also of line, and it must unavoidably condense in an abstract way stitch by stitch. As with her installations in which the threads are spanned in the room like a net and intersect at geometric angles, at her sewing machine the artist can only draw in a geometrically regular "staccato". This is not immediately visible everywhere, it is most clearly seen with some of her more sparsely embroidered works (e.g. fig. p. 56 and p. 73), in which the coloured stitching obviously deviates from the topographic lines in order to "go its own way". And yet with other landscapes the embroiderer becomes a "painter" who precisely follows the sweep of a mountain knoll in plausible colours between green and blue and models it in an enchanting interplay of light and shadow (fig. p. 55). Some of the black-and-white prints with their island-like patches of colour are, if anything, reminiscent of early photographs which were selectively coloured by hand. Such a "non finito" is especially stimulating to our imagination and calls out for individual completion. The embroidery seldom covers the whole format. One example is a close-up view in differentiated shades of green showing an alpine terrain interspersed with rocks and vegetation (fig. p. 76). The picture appears like a finely woven carpet that almost makes us forget that it is based on a photograph. The extremes are paradoxically reconciled in the combination of fast photography and weeks of embroidery.

Orientation and longing
As different as Iris Hutegger's landscapes appear to be, we have a constant impulse to orientate and locate ourselves in them as if we were standing in them physically. A primitive instinct? An urge for survival? This primary existential quest is further intensified by the fact that the selected depictions, often manipulated with deletions or additions, give no kind of indications of real places. Like lost hikers in the lonely mountains we ask, "Where am I? How do I find my way?" It is remarkable with what fervour we still hope to find "our" landscape in even the boldest abstractions.

The varying reception that her works find with the public in different countries aroused Iris Hutegger's interest in landscape as a cultural influence and individual memory picture. She observed, for example, that "people linger in front of familiar pictures considerably longer. If there is previous knowledge of the depicted landscape, a small stimulus from colour and structure in combination with the black-and-white picture is enough to trigger an illusion of reality in the viewer."[5] The familiar landscapes actually become our homeland and also shape our later topographical preferences. These often determine whether we can feel at home quickly or only slowly in a new location.

Such research reflects the serious angle from which Iris Hutegger sees art as a means to knowledge. It is also important for her to clarify terms: "For me landscape and nature are two completely different concepts, if not even independent terms. I think that looking at the landscape only became possible when a distance slid between man and nature."[6] In fact landscape is one of the most recent genres in painting as an independent form of expression. It was with the Enlightenment that landscape first took on significance and it reached its heights with German Romanticism and later with Impressionism. The mostly urban-dwelling painters sought out the countryside as an alternative world and painting outdoors became taken for granted as artistic practice. After landscape had only been acceptable as a background motif for centuries, in the 19th century it rapidly developed into the public's favourite genre—and has remained so until today. Since Denis Diderot references have been made at various times to the connection between the popularity of painted landscapes and the increasing remoteness from nature of their buyers. It is a telling fact that the painterly expression of the idyll flourished from the middle of the 19th century at a time when industrialisation, technology and urbanisation were in full swing.[7]

Distancing, alienation, uncertainty
The longings connected with the genre of landscape, and which attract the public to such exhibitions, are critically scrutinised by Iris Hutegger. When she, for the time being, chooses the alpine region as a basis for her landscapes, the Austrian-born artist is turning to familiar topography. However, in the production of her works she does much to distance herself from what is seen in them as her home country. The origin of her most idiosyncratic technique of embroidering photographs is also telling: it was in fact exasperation and rage that led her to put one of her photographs under the sewing machine—in order to get to grips with a beautiful souvenir picture that appeared phoney to her. Already around 2004/2005, at the same time as her thread installations, black-and-white photographs were appearing that showed clear traces of being scratched. The artist writes: "Landscapes as spaces that are

no longer *located*. Landscapes as spaces that are no longer *seasoned*. / Damage to the surface such as cuts or scratch marks create a new picture. / Damage and creation rolled into one."[8]

The process of alienation of her current landscapes already begins with her printing the original colour photographs on black-and-white photographic paper. The various light values present in classical black-and-white photography, fully focused and differentiated, now appear to flow together as in a painting. Sometimes the photographs appear like soft charcoal or pencil drawings. Although the artist actually uses these techniques to supplement her photographs, they can hardly, or not at all, be distinguished from the original print. Another form of conscious distancing is the long period of time she allows to pass before reworking the photographs that she took in Austria, Switzerland, Greece, Iceland and the United States. In doing so she hopes to forget the relevant memories. Only in this way can she see the landscapes freshly and embroider them with new colours. Her own invented palette is thus preceded by a double deletion of natural colouring: on the one hand by printing a colour film on black-and-white photographic paper and on the other with the process of forgetting.

Deleting and overwriting are practices of the electronic age. Nevertheless Iris Hutegger deliberately uses old techniques for her landscapes: analogue photography with classical silver gelatine prints, drawing, gouache and embroidery. When she prefers analogue to digital photography she decides for the freedom always to be able to control her tools and use them for her artistic purposes. The sensuous and lively expression of her works relates directly to the traces of time becoming visible during the creative process: from close up we can follow the individual stitches of her embroidery just as clearly as the visible brush strokes of a painting or the lines of a drawing.

Trompe-l'œil, abstraction and reality
Nevertheless the old techniques do not lead back to a conventional landscape picture, even if the works continue the long tradition of trompe-l'œil with their astounding harmonisation of different media. Examples of this genre do not only amaze us with their stupendous technique; philosophical thought is concealed behind their visible virtuosity: discovering the trick of the eye diverts the gaze from what is depicted and opens the eye for other things. With Iris Hutegger's works too, the motifs lose more and more meaning during the course of looking at them.

With the increasing confusion about how to interpret these apparently similar landscapes—nothing but landscapes—we look for formal regularities without really finding them: how are the pictures composed? Where are the coloured spaces? How is spatiality evoked? And where is the viewer's place? The relevant answers are often connected to effects and atmospheres: radiant or dull, threatening or enchanting, the feelings evoked primarily find expression via the palette. With longer viewing one notices how abstract many of the landscapes appear: sharply cut mountain silhouettes are set under the blank white of a sky (fig. p. 55 and p. 56), blue and violet ink ribbons are laid in the billow of gentle hill ranges (fig. p. 57). In a portrait format a vermillion red flows towards us finding its way through a bed of boulders and bringing to mind less the blooming of alpine flora than a stream of blood (fig. p. 67). There are several reasons why even the most unnatural colours still fit, apparently harmoniously, in the illusionistic terrain: on the one hand the artist respects the horizontal line with her sewing and emphasises the silhouettes of mountains with denser stitching, on the other she responds to existing structures in specific ways. These include both blending and conscious contrasting: whereas in one place she radically and uninhibitedly sews over a picture surface with a colourful palette of orange, wine red, light blue and violet finding plausible expression for the rank growth of Mediterranean macchia (fig. p. 68), in another she sensitively continues the pebbled ground of a sparse surface with coloured dots (fig. p. 42). The plastic appearance of the textile areas, which emerge physically lucent, also contributes to the astonishingly plausible effect: their material quality suggests naturalness and makes us want to touch the soft forms. And precisely because we seem to be able to grasp these coloured yarns we no longer have to grasp them mentally and question them. Iris Hutegger's works thus teach us to distinguish between naturalness and reality. Because what has an effect on us, what touches and moves us, need not necessarily be natural, even when the motifs play with the idea of the natural. Pure looking is made possible, a slow, almost devotional process of immersion. In this sense her landscaped abstractions resemble Nordic late-Gothic devotional pictures.

Landscape as a genre does not only enable coloured abstraction of the natural but also a basic questioning of natural atmospheres as a mirror to universal human feelings. As such, Iris Hutegger's landscapes can be related to German Romantic art. There is in fact a series of works which, with their melancholy expression, continue the Romantic tradition. Several strikingly dark works are noteworthy: whereas the artist embroiders a small-format mountain landscape very densely with black and yellow threads and darkens the sky with pencil, as if a heavy storm were about to break (fig. p. 71), in another work she completely covers the sky with black paint to make the terrain beneath it appear all the more glaring. She contributes to the further alienation of this almost apocalyptic-looking scene with most curious shades of colour between violet, light blue and orange (fig. p. 75). In contrast, the picture of a mountain lake between hills and scarp slopes appears magical (fig. p. 45): everything in this largely uncoloured landscape is graphically soft, light and bright. And where the artist still found certain parts of the photograph too hard, she brightened them up with white thread or obliterated them. The magic inherent in this silver-toned landscape once again connects with our uncertainty about fact and effect: am I seeing actual colours in the grey picture or am I just imagining them? And aren't the light values of a black-and-white print alone enough to seem coloured?

**Being-in-the-world:
landscape as existential picture**
With the question as to what distinguishes Iris Hutegger's landscapes from works of German Romanticism and what her contemporary contribution represents within the tradition of existential "mental studies", we can return to the "inter esse" mentioned at the beginning, which is different to the conventional exchange between artist, artwork and viewer. This being-between is in fact characterised by communication from all sides, in which the artist does not only act creatively but just as often reacts, in that when sewing she must always engage with something that is already there. And the viewer is no longer merely a passive onlooker but rather—as in the experience of an installation—a participant perceiving with all the senses.

Are Iris Hutegger's pictures landscapes at all? Instead of motifs their titles are just numbers: the first two digits stand for the year the work was completed and the following two for the month; the final digits are the respective work number. "Landscape" is primarily an art historical concept, a cultural invention that says more about our existential being-in-the-world, our world view, than about a specific place. Iris Hutegger's landscapes also do not show a homeland in a conventional sense, even if she began her pictures precisely where she felt at home, in the alpine world of her (chosen) home country. In spite of this, the question of feeling safe and sound is pivotal. Her works, which appear three-dimensional and are starkly aimed at the viewer, ultimately turn around the basic question of space and positioning. In it, like her example Alberto Giacometti, she combines the artistic question of the representability of reality with the search for an up-to-date picture of human existence. Particularly in the age of virtuality, which is making orientation increasingly difficult, Iris Hutegger does not want to foster any illusions. At the same time she applies herself to the suggestion of sensuous reality with such dedication that we are at least able to understand her landscapes as a model world for scenic experience.

The body as a possible homeland
However, ultimately her eye is directed less towards perception of the world, which is becoming increasingly impenetrable and deceptive, than towards the body which nevertheless wants to perceive this world with all the senses. It is not only the importance of handwork as a relation to reality but also the haptic presence and effect of the work which induces a state of physical alertness in the viewer. Iris Hutegger has already speculated that the body could be a possible location of homeland in a text about Chiharu Shiota: the body becomes a storage device for stories, experiences and memories which condense there, it becomes a container "in which all times exist simultaneously".[9] This description can also be applied to the picture-bodies of her landscapes.

"Homeland" has in many ways become mouldy, a slogan for politics and advertising, at a time in which a specific relationship to home country has become increasingly difficult and indeed more suspect. When Iris Hutegger invents landscapes, which ultimately remain alien to us, she is responding to an increased feeling of rootlessness. However, in her works are reflected values in which footholds can be found: work as fulfilment, difference as enrichment and sensuousness as life energy.

1   Iris Hutegger, *Geschichten. Netzwerk, Betten Le_rstellen im Werk von Chiharu Shiota*, intermediate diploma II, FHBB HGK Basel, Dept. Fine Art/Media Art, unpublished typescript, August 2004, p. 6.
2   Iris Hutegger, *Ich bin Bildhauerin*, unpublished typescript, October 2014.
3   Interview with Elena Monzo, Milan, and Iris Hutegger, Füllinsdorf, April 2015, unpublished typescript, p. 6.
4   See footnote 1.—In 2002 Iris Hutegger saw an installation by Chiharu Shiota at the exhibition *Another World—Zwölf Bettgeschichten* at Kunstmuseum Luzern. She was so deeply impressed that in 2004 she devoted her intermediate diploma at Basel to the work. However, in contrast to Shiota, who used 20 beds for her Luzern installation, Hutegger has consistently dispensed with the integration of everyday objects in her own thread installations.
5   Iris Hutegger, *Ich bin Bildhauerin,* see footnote 2, p. 3.
6   Loc cit., p. 2.
7   See Rolf Wedewer, Jens Christian Jensen (Ed.), *Die Idylle. Eine Bildform im Wandel. Zwischen Hoffnung und Wirklichkeit. 1750–1930,* Cologne: DuMont, 1987.—Barbara Eschenburg, *Landschaft in der deutschen Malerei*, Munich: C.H. Beck, 1987 (here esp. the chapter "Industrialisierung und Naturverklärung", pp. 165–181).
8   Book "Fotografien 2004/2005" from an eight-part dossier with work groups from 2003–2005, artist's publication, 2005.
9   See motto, footnote 1.

The Thread Running Through It[1]
Iris Hutegger's Embroidered Photographs

KARINE TISSOT

Just as painters squeeze the tubes of color pigments onto their palettes to get the particular shade they are looking for, and sculptors remove portions of the material they are working on to lend form a solid reality, Iris Hutegger employs specific protocols that involve alternately tearing apart and piecing back together in the singular practice that is sewing. This Austrian-born visual artist is creating a body of work that she calls photography, drawing, painting, and occasionally sculpture. It also puts her in contact with the sewing machine. Photo paper as a support is the thing that brings the work to light. She views it physically, in the resistance it poses. A story has to form, a timeline take shape, a new image be created thanks to thread.

Ariadne's thread is in such a state
From the ancient mythological imagination to our day and age, the symbolism of the thread has not changed. Through the vital link it crystallizes life's direction. In Greek mythology, the thread of life is spun from the distaff of the Moirai,[2] the Fates, the goddesses that preside over destiny. Birth is represented by the distaff that Clotho holds; the thread of events is measured out by the spindle that Lachesis works; and death is symbolized by the shears Atropos wields. As for Ariadne, the daughter of Minos unwinds her thread so that Theseus can find the way out of the maze, while Penelope comes up with a trick to continually weave, unweave, and reweave her tapestry in order to put time, and her fate, on hold.

To disconnect while embroidering, to leave behind the surrounding world, one's problems and reality for a time. Long a way out for women and a symbol of education for young ladies who, with their trousseau, could weave a future for themselves as prospective wives, needlework carries within it a silent world of storytelling, tension, and sublimation which takes different forms according to the time and culture. And having exclusively served sewing and embroidery for centuries, thread in the field of contemporary art is more or less indebted to that story. It is by turns figurative and abstract, but most certainly hungry for ideas. That is, it makes it possible to articulate, express, or work the image far beyond domestic, functional, or decorative tradition. Mixing various media to better "break down the walls" of tradition, Hutegger's work is definitely part of that idea of openness. The production space is meditative and time a creative element.

Nowadays, it is obvious that the gestures of weaving and plaiting, strictly speaking, no longer fall under the category of the handicraft of yore but have been ritualized, giving rise to creations of a different stripe, like the monumental networks of threads devised by Chiharu Shiota,[3] or the dense assemblages of colored fiber fashioned by Sheila Hicks.[4] It is also as an Arachnidan that the Argentine artist Tomás Saraceno[5] illustrates his theories of clouds, while the Mexican artist Gabriel Dawe[6] weaves colorful compositions. In a more minimalist vein, Fred Sandback[7] left behind a conceptual body of work made up of a few lines, taking the removal of material in sculpture to the extreme in order to experience its materiality as far as possible. In a way Hutegger was following in his footsteps when she experimented with spatial drawing in the following installations, *Freier Eintritt an allen Tagen* in 2009, *Doors and Stairs* in 2010, and *Auch, Noch* in 2011.[8]

In another genre, threads and nets tangle and twist in the patched-together works of Annette Messager,[9] who explains that she has "always been interested in devalued arts. As a woman, [she] was already a devalued artist. Belonging to a minority, [she is] drawn to so-called minor values and objects. That probably gives rise to [her] taste for popular art, proverbs, naïve art, maxims, fairytales, the art of the everyday, embroidery, movies."[10]

Finally, alongside the field of contemporary art, yarn bombing, also known as knit graffiti, has found a place for itself in the public thoroughfare for a decade or so now as a way of humanizing the urban fabric, coloring the asphalt, and making a so-called minor art—knitting, crocheting, sewing—into a collective and often anonymous force in our individualist societies. This urban knitting might be understood as the popular counterpart of the baroque artworks created by the artist Joana Vasconcelos,[11] which mix fabrics, clothing, and doilies with wonderfully complicated embroidery; or the wool paintings done by Rosemarie Trockel;[12] or the textile pieces of Anni Albers,[13] who managed to marry geometrical abstraction and vernacular practices connected with extra-Western cultures.

The applied thread
When the thread closely adheres to the support, as in Hutegger's practice with her photographs, it assumes different aspects. It becomes drawing, for example, in the portraits done by Sandrine Pelletier,[14] a scar in Annegret Soltau's portraits,[15] a grafted-on addition in the work of Cathryn Boch,[16] and color in the hyperrealist compositions of Cayce Zavaglia.[17] At other times, it is illustration in the half-ink half-cotton line jointly drawn by Isabelle Pralong[18] and Aurélie William Levaux,[19] or ornament in the enhanced 1950s photos of Hinke Schreuders.[20] Similarly, it can play up suppleness in a sort of loose floating, which Aglaia Haritz[21] makes abundant use of, or as Maria Lai[22] employed in her illegible handwriting, which is no less evocative of moods and thoughts. On the other hand, it can also show tension, as in the string masks that Martine Birobent[23] crocheted with a firm hand to both muzzle and clothe a range of dolls, or in the "mummifying" of objects that Alice Anderson[24] does using copper wire. And the abstract pieces of Pierrette Bloch[25] incorporate traditionally female skills, reconnecting with buried memories through the use of thread in a range of forms.

No matter, thread isn't only a women's thing today. The *Mappa*,[26] Alighiero e Boetti's embroidered planispheres that were first done in 1971 and continued to be produced until his death,[27] figure among the most famous of the Arte Povera artist's output. Meanwhile, Michael Raedecker[28] puts embroidery front and center in his work, turning to a freely applied stitching structuring the surface of his paintings to create drip and brushstroke effects.

"Thread in the photograph"[29]
Like Raedecker—after first developing three-dimensional experiments[30] like those mentioned above—Hutegger now uses an initial medium, photography, to which she affixes a thread. The introduction of the technique of sewing—without any deliberate feminist claims or feminine connotation—is discreet, tenuous, like some subtle bit of coquetry. The artist demands attention, curiosity, and concentration on the part of viewers if they don't wish to miss the point of the work. By moving in closer, taking the time to look, really stopping, they will discover the slight relief of the thread and its gentle colored harmonies[31] that skillfully contrast with the black-and-white landscape backgrounds.

Traces of a "shimmering passage" or a covering of vegetation? The color accents are indeed hard to pin down. You might think you recognize here and there the soft green pillows of *Scleranthus uniflorus* on photographed troughs, that type of moss we are forever looking to eliminate in Europe whereas it is a choice green plant in the Land of the Rising Sun. Witness the gardens of Saiho-ji, also known as Koke-dera—or the "moss temple"—which contain over 120 different species. In Hutegger's compositions that diversity could explain the variations that run from red to green and may even verge on blue-green occasionally. But whatever the palette, the combinations of color threads offer no help for identifying landscapes which inevitably risk looking foreign, be they in Iceland, the United States, Austria, or Switzerland, simply because the original hues are altered.

Views of the mind
Although she is familiar with Austrian mountains and the Swiss Alps,[32] Hutegger "never reveals the sites of [her] photographs." Through the filter of black and white, the photo treats everything uniformly, the ruggedness of cliffs or the gentle grace of hilly curves, the surfaces of water and the rocks in the middle of valleys, the meadows and the forests, pointing less to the subjective and animated forces of romantic art than to mental landscapes, views of the mind. The stitching vigorously follows the photographic shapes printed in black and white even though they were recorded in color. A technical effect that in reality reduces the contrasts, draping a soft veil of camaieu gray over the landscapes.

On these shades of gray and evanescent horizons, the thread draws nervous, insistent, thick lines. It catches on stone, the ground, yet never extends to the sky or bodies of water. Under the pressure of the needle, the paper suffers and timidly gives way here and there. Lines take over the surface with threads that are woven in depth, the material indifferently divided between the front and back of the photograph. As such, the stitching points up a play of the visible and the hidden, presence and absence, appearance and disappearance, through that length of thread that revives the idea of color and at the same time can only be seen on the front of the photo. A singular piece of work that expresses doubts about the compactness of reality and the immutable order of things through a subtle play of restless scratched lines. Like an inkling of uncertainty. Part of the landscape is insidiously gnawed away, and what is solid is nibbled at from one end to the other by the threads.

Perhaps this is how Hutegger's mixed compositions encourage contemplation in a suspended moment. The choice of a restricted palette limited to a few hues that are always dominated by the black and white of the background also plays a part in that. It makes it possible to reveal, as in traditional Chinese painting, the infinite variety of a range of colors. That is, in Hutegger's photographs, as in Chinese landscapes of long ago, there is indeed no need to express color in color. Where more or less dense India ink allowed artists to conjure up the world, Hutegger's work offers a universal mental depiction of landscapes without lingering over the details of the nature being depicted. No color or particular framing ever suggests the anecdotal, the specific—not a flower, not a blade of grass—on the contrary, the artist weaves lines or flat patches of color that are more or less distinct from one another and resonate with an idea of abstraction, dodging the similarity with the photo's reality: "When I do stitching on a photograph, I never stitch grass, lichen, or flowers. I work the structures, the photographic material, lines that can trigger memories. Sewing for me has a high degree of abstraction." In this regard, the views that are selected are deliberately unspectacular, opening onto a broad field of possible interpretations.

Stepping back
Just as it was done in the Middle Kingdom as well, Hutegger takes care to step back from her motif. The idea is to forget the skill in order to gain a new burst of creativity. Comparison with the culture of the other continent allows us to emphasize concepts like inspiration or rhythm, the cardinal parameters of

an intuitive approach that dismisses any sort of analysis in danger of confining the work to a particular discourse. To take the parallel with traditional China further, one might compare Hutegger's *photography* with the *Chinese brush*—both of which produce forms, structure, broad lines—and the *thread* with *ink*—which add "wrinkles," modulations, shadows, and light in compositions. Components that are inseparable from one another, just as flesh and bones or mountains and lakes are.

Through her work in the end, Iris Hutegger applies a recurrent theme, that is, through more or less large landscapes she maintains her views, which stand midway between anonymity and "individuality." She who can no longer separate photography from the thread stresses that "the work must be one." The artist goes on to say, "I'm interested in landscapes generally," photographing permanently an idea of the world. "For me the landscape is more a mental space. It is made up of neither a beginning nor an end, it is quite simply framed by the image one makes of it at a given moment." It is based on nature in order to find the creative force of the world and capture "the elusive" once again—which is so dear to the Chinese—or maybe even "the force of the vital spirit."

An act of destruction

One then thinks of the paper, a surface that the needle of the sewing machine comes to pierce. Looking closely, one is divided between appreciating the refined work and almost tactilely perceiving the idea of a scar, a gash running through the photograph. It is a sensation that is reinforced by small holes that have been made in the paper and left more or less large. If stitching, like painting, is a working texture, it does have one particularity, i.e., it works the front of the support as well as the reverse and the space in between. The stitching simultaneously fixes and separates the paper. It reconstitutes an autonomous material, constrains the support, lends it volume. The needle used by Hutegger is mechanical, loud; it doesn't simply glide over a fabric, doesn't assemble a piece, it mistreats the photographic paper and creates lacelike effects in areas. Following the "thread" of the outlines as they turn, accelerate, and double back, it marks the sheet with a series of stitches that are densely packed to an extreme degree. The paper shows and retains this mark of fiber within the fiber. There is a form of violence that is imposed on the support, a risk undertaken vis-à-vis the pre-existing image that is eventually altered. With the sewing machine, the tension is permanent both literally and figuratively. Which explains the use of synthetic thread. It is more resistant than cotton, which easily breaks in this kind of use.[33]

We should recall that in Hutegger's work, this use of "embroidered photography" originally sprang from an act of destruction. Disappointed by the photography she was producing at the time, Hutegger grew so annoyed one day—she was still a student then—that she went at one with a vengeance. But before getting rid of it, "noticing the sewing machine, [she] immediately grabbed it, with no ulterior motive or thought in mind, to destroy everything." Once she had soothed her nerves the artist was surprised to find herself looking carefully at the results. The accident brought to light an unexpected texture offering the chance to steer her practice of the medium in a new direction—"what the needle destroyed was simultaneously recreated by the thread." Thread now made it possible not only to weave webs and thus play up transparent areas in places, but also to thoroughly cover other parts at the risk of modifying the image entirely or in part. For Hutegger, "the most important factor in this manipulation lies in the fact that photography shifts to the status of an image. Through this process, photography fuses with the idea of drawing (through line), painting (through color), and sculpture (through the addition of material)." The artist's violent act would now be deliberately mastered and contained in a form of estheticism that avoids all showy overstatement that might otherwise take the form of patches, engravings, grafts, or patchworks.

In praise of silence and slowness
After the noisy back and forth of the machine, silence reigns once again in the artist's studio. For Hutegger's photos have already been developed in silence in the darkroom. "It would be impossible to work on digital photography," the artist points out, all too aware that her work would resonate differently in the bygone Analogical Age. The result of her compositions also helps the viewer to achieve a silent tranquility. "The landscape I record in my photographs is always immaculate, devoid of any path or other sign of civilization." It is about mountains but even more about minerals and plants which are, with their immobility, the very setting of these words by Paul Virilio, "For a very long time... I have claimed to be 'terrestrial,' and I have explained that we should replace the term 'human' by 'terrestrial.' That is justified all the more when we realize that the term 'human' comes from 'humus,' in other words earth. I think that in an age when we are losing our connection with the earth, reducing the world to nothing through speed, progress, acceleration, it might be time for us to recognize that we are terrestrials. We are part of the animal species, we are animated beings. That is, we move about, unlike plants and especially minerals."[34]

Running counter to a time that is hastily spent nowadays, Hutegger combines several timeframes in an image that is structured in depth. From the ancient peaks captured in mere fractions of a second by the camera, to the color image slowed down by the darkroom developing process, to the lightning-quick passage of a precise and resolute sewing machine needle—not to mention the choice of the color to embroider, which can sometimes take months—time in her work is articulated in both the past and the present, "Each line is now the actual experience with its own innate history. It does not illustrate—it is the sensation of its own realization,"[35] as Cy Twombly once put it. Finally, we read linear time symbolically in the thread that spools out as it is created and leads us to our end according to the precepts of mythology.

Like women doing embroidery, Hutegger is focused on her work. She is concentrated on an activity that both occupies the mind and frees it from the turbulences of thought. Nevertheless, the exercise this visual artist is engaged in is a far cry from the manual activity that allows one to unwind as it captures and holds one's attention. She works on several photographs at the same time, and this allows her to advance in a stimulating way their respective compositions, which of course are also developing in parallel. Work on one benefits the other and vice versa. The piece is put back on the loom "as the ideas are spun out." Each composition suggests its own rules, "no green color," "only green," "follow the shape of the Alps," and so on. It is a way to avoid diluting the artist's intentions while enabling her to focus on a precise project.

The work is not easy, like "threading" a needle. At times the piece is hanging by a "thread." And some are poised on the razor's edge: if the result proves unsuitable, the thread is cut and the piece completely destroyed.

"Losing the thread"
Built on the identity of the gesture, Hutegger's work absolutely questions the heritage and influences of

the ornamental repertory of the "home," be it consciously or unconsciously, since adding with a needle an ornamentation, whatever its nature, to a pre-existing background is the very definition of embroidery, an art form that has been employed for ages. Yet the artist's work basically questions a contemporary art that lies at the point where the beautiful and the useful meet, mixing the codes of art, design, and industry. This reminds us that for decades now, visceral connections have formed between the worlds of art and textiles in the excitement and ferment of modernity. Taking up material and thread certain artists wrought profound changes in the notion of artmaking in needlework and vice versa. Likewise, the forgotten works of the applied arts, which were never viewed as works of art, have regained considerable expressive and contemporary power since the last century. Iris Hutegger's work is squarely on that path, imbued with the wish to show the same calm that contemplating a real landscape affords. She does this thanks to threads, in lines and in relief, which enable her to elaborate worlds that are distinct, novel, improbable, and simultaneously familiar and uncertain. Finally, it is worth recalling here that against the claims of mastery, it is the uncertainties that tell us that art consists in "losing the thread" at times, the one Ariadne provided, the one that lends meaning and direction to the labyrinth and to life—and that the real labyrinth isn't the one that Daedalus built, it is the one confronting us when our eye wanders over an image.

1 "Du fil dans les idées" (literally "thread in the ideas" and figuratively the thread running through one's ideas) is the original title of the present essay in French and the name of an exhibition that ran at the Théâtre de la Tournelle in Orbe, from 7 to 29 November 2015. Mounted by the Centre d'art contemporain of Yverdon-les-Bains, the show was curated by Karine Tissot. The following artists took part: Martine Birobent, Joëlle Flumet, Liliana Gassiot, Aglaia Haritz, Stefanie Holler, Iris Hutegger, Aurélie William Levaux, Sandrine Pelletier, Isabelle Pralong, Sophie Schmidt, and Garance Tschumi.
2 Called the Moirai (from *moira*, destiny, fate) by the ancient Greeks and the Parcae (*pario*, to bear, to give birth to, to beget) by the Romans.
3 Chiharu Shiota was born in 1972 in Japan; she has lived and worked in Berlin since 1996. She represented Japan at the 2015 Venice Biennial of Contemporary Art with a piece that featured threads of varying dimensions strung throughout the space she was allotted.
4 Sheila Hicks was born in 1934 in the United States; she has lived and worked in Paris since 1964. In 2014 she exhibited her assemblages at the Palais de Tokyo in Paris.
5 Tomás Saraceno was born in 1973 in Argentina, where he lives and works today.
6 Gabriel Dawe was born in 1973 in Mexico City; he lives and works in Dallas.
7 The American artist Fred Sandback (1943–2003).
8 *Freier Eintritt an allen Tagen,* 2009, was created for the show "Landscapes," Studio Rondo, Graz, Austria; *Doors and Stairs,* 2010, for the show "Bitte, Nehmen Sie Platz!" artforum Spitzbart, Germany; and *Auch, Noch,* 2011, for "RegioArtSkulptur," Rehmann Museum, Laufenburg, Switzerland. These are all installations in which Hutegger's thread became a drawing in the venue.
9 Annette Messager was born in 1943 in Berck-sur-Mer, France; she lives and works near Paris.
10 Bernard Mercadé, 2007, "L'artiste et ses doubles," *Beaux-Arts, special Annette Messager edition* 9 (2007), pp. 8–13.
11 Joana Vasconcelos was born in 1971 in Paris; she lives and works in Lisbon.
12 Rosemarie Trockel was born in 1952 in Germany, where she lives and works.
13 The German-born American artist Anni Albers (1899–1994).
14 Sandrine Pelletier was born in 1976 in Lausanne; she lives and works in Geneva and Brussels.
15 Annegret Soltau was born in 1946 in Germany; she lives and works in Darmstadt.
16 Cathryn Boch was born in 1968 in Strasbourg; she lives and works in Marseille.
17 Cayce Zavaglia was born in 1971 in the United States, where she lives and works.
18 Isabelle Pralong was born in 1967 in Sion; she lives and works in Geneva. See the following footnote.
19 Aurélie William Levaux was born in 1981 in Belgium, where she lives and works. With Isabelle Pralong, she published *Prédictions* in 2011 (Éditions Atrabile), illustrating on pieces

of cloth with a ballpoint pen and needle various moments from the Peter Handke play of the same name.
20 Hinke Schreuders was born in 1969; she lives and works in the Netherlands.
21 Aglaia Haritz was born in 1978 in the Tessin region of Switzerland, where she lives and works. For several years now, she has pursued a traveling art project throughout the Arab world with the Moroccan artist Abdelaziz Zerrou on the condition of women in these regions. The project is called *Brodeuses d'actualité* (literally Embroiderers of Current Events).
22 The Italian artist Maria Lai (1919–2013).
23 The French-Canadian artist Martine Birobent (1955–2016).
24 Alice Anderson was born in 1976 in London, where she lives and works.
25 Pierrette Bloch was born in 1928 in Paris, where she lives and works.
26 "Concentrates of time," since they occasionally required up to five years of labor by Afghani weavers or embroiderers. The artist had a long experience with the practice of subcontracting his work.
27 The Italian artist Alighiero e Boetti (1940–1994).
28 Michael Raedecker was born in 1963 in Amsterdam; he lives and works in London.
29 The original subhead here, *De fil en photographie*, alludes to the French expression *de fil en aiguille*, "one thing leads to another." ["Thread" is naturally a (sometimes untranslatable) thread running throughout the text—Trans.]
30 See note 8.
31 Hutegger occasionally employs gouache or pencil highlights in addition to embroidery.
32 Hutegger grew up in Austria in the middle of the Alps. When she arrived in Switzerland, she settled first in the canton of Graubünden and then Lucerne, two regions that are indeed surrounded by mountains. Today, living in Basel, she lives one hour by train from the mountains, which offers her a kind of distance from that motif, moreover.
33 We should note that Hutegger uses cotton nonetheless for black areas since color is denser in a different way.
34 *Culture mobile, penser la société du numérique*, "Paul Virilio, Terra Nova," interview conducted by Yvon Le Mignan and Ariel Kyrou, 17 November 2008.
35 Cy Twombly, *L'Esperienza moderna* 2 (August-September 1957), p.32.

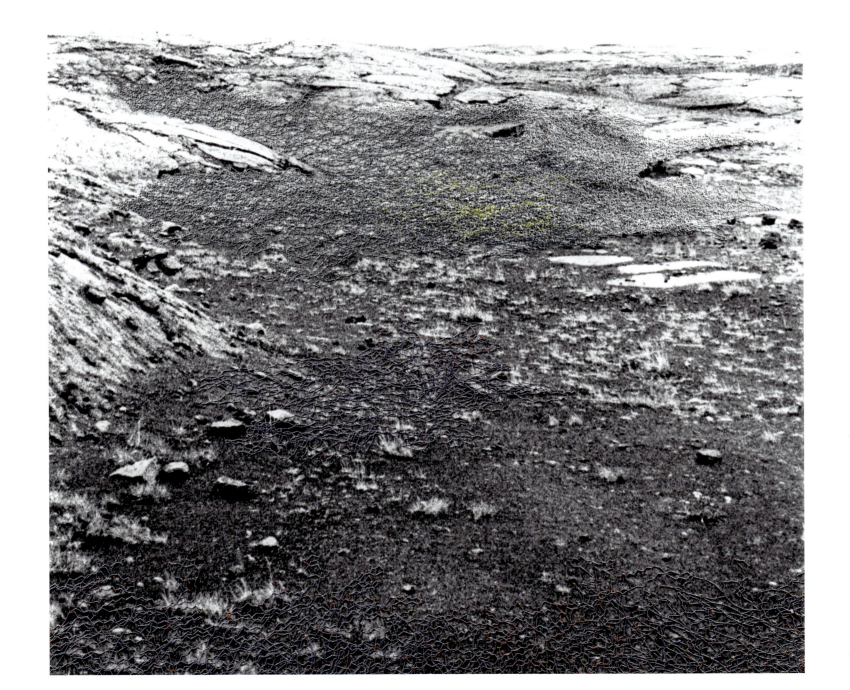

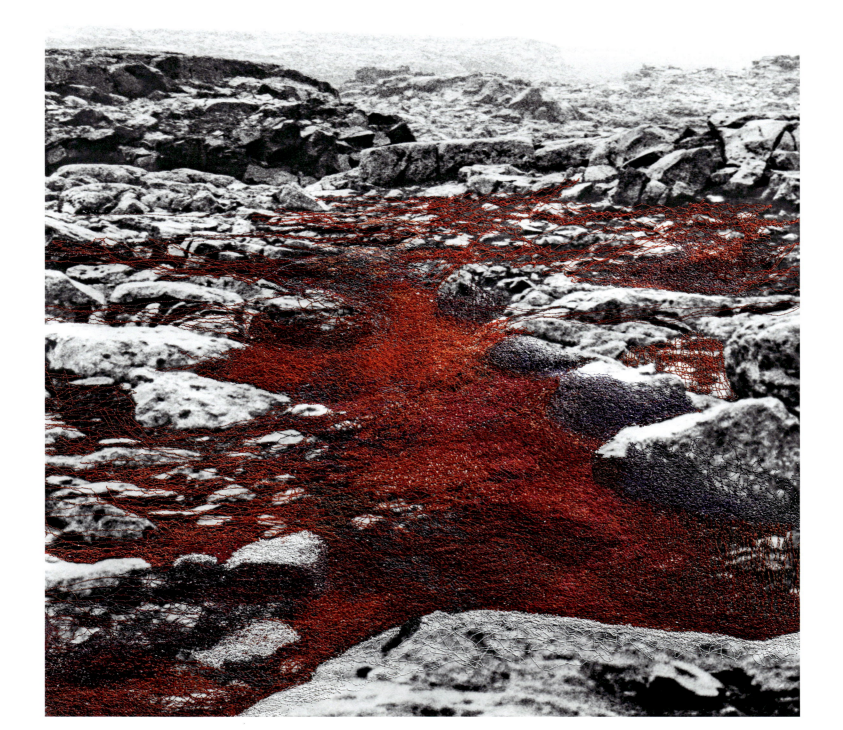

Anhang — Appendix

Liste der Abbildungen — List of Works

41 1602 – 213. 2016
71,6 × 46,5 cm
Analoge Fotografie, Silbergelatine-Abzug, Faden —
Analogue photography, silver gelatine print, thread

42 1510 – 222. 2015
37 × 54,8 cm
Analoge Fotografie, Silbergelatine-Abzug, Faden —
Analogue photography, silver gelatine print, thread
R. & P. Herzog, Basel

43 1604 – 366. 2016
28 × 40,8 cm
Analoge Fotografie, Silbergelatine-Abzug, Faden —
Analogue photography, silver gelatine print, thread

45 1505 – 324. 2015
58,5 × 89 cm
Analoge Fotografie, Silbergelatine-Abzug, Faden, Grafit —
Analogue photography, silver gelatine print, thread, graphite

47 1603 – 292. 2016
69 × 47,5 cm
Analoge Fotografie, Silbergelatine-Abzug, Faden, Grafit,
Gouache — Analogue photography, silver gelatine print,
thread, gouache

49 1606 – 379. 2016
70 × 45,6 cm
Analoge Fotografie, Silbergelatine-Abzug, Faden —
Analogue photography, silver gelatine print, thread

51 1605 – 406. 2016
33,7 × 21,5 cm
Analoge Fotografie, Silbergelatine-Abzug, Faden —
Analogue photography, silver gelatine print, thread

52 1505 – 585. 2015
36,9 × 55,2 cm
Analoge Fotografie, Silbergelatine-Abzug, Faden —
Analogue photography, silver gelatine print, thread
R. & P. Herzog, Basel

53 1505 – 344. 2015
21,5 × 33,5 cm
Analoge Fotografie, Silbergelatine-Abzug, Faden —
Analogue photography, silver gelatine print, thread

55 1602 – 294. 2016
28 × 40,5 cm
Analoge Fotografie, Silbergelatine-Abzug, Faden —
Analogue photography, silver gelatine print, thread

56 1605 – 380. 2016
36 × 56 cm
Analoge Fotografie, Silbergelatine-Abzug, Faden —
Analogue photography, silver gelatine print, thread

57 1604 – 363. 2016
36 × 56 cm
Analoge Fotografie, Silbergelatine-Abzug, Faden, Grafit —
Analogue photography, silver gelatine print, thread, graphite

59 1512 – 205. 2015
71,5 × 46,5 cm
Analoge Fotografie, Silbergelatine-Abzug, Faden —
Analogue photography, silver gelatine print, thread
Privatbesitz, Brüssel — Private collection, Brussels

61 1512 – 229. 2015
71,2 × 46,4 cm
Analoge Fotografie, Silbergelatine-Abzug, Faden —
Analogue photography, silver gelatine print, thread

63 1512 – 228. 2015
　　71,4 × 46,4 cm
　　Analoge Fotografie, Silbergelatine-Abzug, Faden —
　　Analogue photography, silver gelatine print, thread

65 1602 – 285. 2016
　　70,2 × 47 cm
　　Analoge Fotografie, Silbergelatine-Abzug, Faden —
　　Analogue photography, silver gelatine print, thread

67 1510 – 215. 2015
　　71,6 × 46,3 cm
　　Analoge Fotografie, Silbergelatine-Abzug, Faden —
　　Analogue photography, silver gelatine print, thread
　　R. & P. Herzog, Basel

68 1508 – 348. 2015
　　28 × 41,3 cm
　　Analoge Fotografie, Silbergelatine-Abzug, Faden —
　　Analogue photography, silver gelatine print, thread

69 1603 – 299. 2016
　　28 × 40,6 cm
　　Analoge Fotografie, Silbergelatine-Abzug, Faden —
　　Analogue photography, silver gelatine print, thread

71 1408 – 419. 2014
　　28,2 × 41,3 cm
　　Analoge Fotografie, Silbergelatine-Abzug, Faden, Grafit —
　　Analogue photography, silver gelatine print, thread, graphite
　　Privatbesitz, Schweiz — Private collection, Switzerland

73 1408 – 533. 2014
　　117 × 74,2 cm
　　Analoge Fotografie, Silbergelatine-Abzug, Faden —
　　Analogue photography, silver gelatine print, thread
　　Privatbesitz, Basel — Private collection, Basel

75 1604 – 296. 2016
　　28 × 40,5 cm
　　Analoge Fotografie, Silbergelatine-Abzug, Faden, Gouache —
　　Analogue photography, silver gelatine print, thread, gouache

76 1503 – 509. 2015
　　58,3 × 89,3 cm
　　Analoge Fotografie, Silbergelatine-Abzug, Faden, Grafit —
　　Analogue photography, silver gelatine print, thread, graphite

77 1603 – 358. 2016
　　36,7 × 54,8 cm
　　Analoge Fotografie, Silbergelatine-Abzug, Faden —
　　Analogue photography, silver gelatine print, thread

79 1605 – 381. 2016
　　110 × 73,5 cm
　　Analoge Fotografie, Silbergelatine-Abzug, Faden, Gouache —
　　Analogue photography, silver gelatine print, thread, gouache

Iris Hutegger

Biografie
Biography

1964 Geboren in Schladming, Österreich — Born in Schladming, Austria

1990 Einreise in die Schweiz — Moved to Switzerland

1994–1999 Semesterkurse Figürliches Modellieren — Semester courses in figure modelling
Hochschule für Gestaltung und Kunst, Zürich

1999/2000 Jahreskurs Figürliches Zeichnen — Annual course in figure drawing
Hochschule für Gestaltung und Kunst, Luzern

1999–2000 Jahreskurs Holz-Bildhauerei — Annual course in wood sculpture
Hochschule für Gestaltung und Kunst, Luzern

2001–2002 Vorkurs — Preliminary course
Hochschule für Gestaltung und Kunst Luzern

2002–2005 Fachhochschule Nordwestschweiz
Hochschule für Gestaltung und Kunst, Basel,
Bachelor Bildende Kunst / Medienkunst — B. A. in Fine Art / Media Art

Einzel- und Doppelausstellungen
Single and Double Exhibitions

2005 *Parkplatz in unmittelbarer Nähe*
Ehemalige Baumwollspinnerei Streiff, Aathal, CH

Gegen Abend stürmische Bise aus Westen
Kunstraum Lodypop, Basel

2007 *Please, hold the line*
Dinnerware Artspace, Projects Gallery Tucson, Arizona, USA

2010 *Bitte, nehmen Sie Platz*
spitzbart_FORUMTREPPE®, Oberasbach, DE

In – out
Galerie Kon-temporär, Land Steiermark, Graz, AT
(zusammen mit — together with Daphna Weinstein)

2013 *La montagna incantata*
Galleria Martini & Ronchetti, Genua *

2014 *Ceci n'est pas un paysage*
Galerie Jacques Cerami, Charleroi, BE

2016 *windstill. grün*
Galerie Esther Woerdehoff, Paris

Dans l'œil de l'observateur
Galerie Jacques Cerami, Charleroi, BE

Iris Hutegger und Alice Bailly
Kunstmuseum Solothurn *

* Katalog — catalog

Gruppenausstellungen (Auswahl) —
Group Exhibitions (Selection)

2005 *Regionale*
FABRIKcultur Hegenheim, FR

Diplomausstellung HGK Basel
Kunsthaus Baselland, Muttenz

2007 *What is life, stripped bare?*
Online-Projekt, documenta 12, Kassel (Video-Beitrag)

2009 *Regionale*
FABRIKcultur, Hegenheim, FR

2011 *Regio Art Skulptur*
Museum Rehmann, Laufenburg, CH

2012 *Regionale*
Stapflehus, Weil am Rhein, DE

2013 *Maravee Anima*
Castello di Susans, Udine, IT

Entrée,
Visarte Basel, M 54, Basel

2014 *trovato non veduto*
Ausstellungsraum Klingental, Basel

Paris Photo
Galerie Esther Woerdehoff, Paris

Regionale
E-Werk, Freiburg im Breisgau

Photographie En Pointure
Galleria Whitelabs, Milano

2015 *Du fil dans les idées*
Théâtre de la Tournelle.
In Zusammenarbeit mit dem — In cooperation with
Centre d'art contemporain d'Yverdon-les-Bains, CH

Paris Photo
Galerie Esther Woerdehoff, Paris

Atelierstipendien / Auslandaufenthalte —
Studio Grants / Stays Abroad

November 2006 – Februar 2007:
Aufenthalt — Stay in Tucson, Arizona, USA

Mai – September 2007:
Aufenthalt — Stay in Tucson, Arizona, USA

Januar – Juni 2009:
Atelierstipendium des Landes Steiermark — Studio grant
from the province of Styria, Atelier Rondo, Graz, AT

September – Oktober 2014
Artist in Residenz — Artist in Resindence, Institute of
Gunnar Gunnarsson, Skriðuklaustri, Egilsstaðir, IS

Autoren — Authors

Karine Tissot (* 1974), Studium der Kunstgeschichte in Genf. Langjährige Tätigkeit am Musée d'art et d'histoire Genève und am Musée d'art moderne et contemporain Genève sowie als Dozentin und Kunstkritikerin. Seit 2013 Direktorin des Centre d'art contemporain d'Yverdon-les-Bains, das sie gegründet hat. Zahlreiche Publikationen und Ausstellungen: *Artistes à Genève, de 1400 à nos jours* (2010); *Les Objets de l'art contemporain* (2011); *Trait Papier, un essai sur le dessin contemporain* (2012); *De la Géométrie sur les murs (2013); Hadrien Dussoix (2014); Hotel Ausland (2014); Keliuaisikiqs – Karim Noureldin* (2015); *Totchic – Elisabeth Llach* (2016).

Christoph Vögele (* 1957), Studium der Kunstgeschichte und Germanistik in Zürich, Paris und Albany (USA). 1992 Dissertation über Niklaus Stoecklin. 1987–1997 freier Kunstkritiker, Kurator und Autor. 2000–2008 Präsident der künstlerischen Kommission des Istituto Svizzero di Roma. Seit 1998 Konservator des Kunstmuseums Solothurn. Zahlreiche Ausstellungen und Publikationen sowohl zur Schweizer Gegenwartskunst (u. a. Silvie Defraoui, Alexander Hahn, Daniela Keiser, Ingeborg Lüscher, Mario Sala, Adrian Schiess, Albrecht Schnider, Roman Signer, Uwe Wittwer) wie auch zur Schweizer Kunstgeschichte (u. a. Cuno Amiet, Giovanni Giacometti, Ferdinand Hodler, Sophie Taeuber-Arp, Félix Vallotton).

Karine Tissot (* 1974), studied art history in Geneva. Worked for many years at the Musée d'art et d'histoire Genève and at the Musée d'art moderne et contemporain Genève and as a lecturer and art critic. Since 2013 director of the Centre d'art contemporain d'Yverdon-les-Bains, which she founded. Numerous publications and exhibitions: *Artistes à Genève, de 1400 à nos jours* (2010); *Les Objets de l'art contemporain* (2011); *Trait Papier, un essai sur le dessin contemporain* (2012); *De la Géométrie sur les murs* (2013); *Hadrien Dussoix* (2014); *Hotel Ausland* (2014); *Keliuaisikiqs – Karim Noureldin* (2015); *Totchic – Elisabeth Llach* (2016).

Christoph Vögele (*1957), studied art history and German studies in Zurich, Paris and Albany (USA). 1992 Dissertation on Niklaus Stoecklin. 1987–1997, freelance art critic, curator and author. 2000–2008 president of the art committee of the Istituto Svizzero di Roma. Since 1998 curator at Kunstmuseum Solothurn. Numerous exhibitions and publications on both contemporary Swiss art (incl. Silvie Defraoui, Alexander Hahn, Daniela Keiser, Ingeborg Lüscher, Mario Sala, Adrian Schiess, Albrecht Schnider, Roman Signer and Uwe Wittwer) and Swiss art history (incl. Cuno Amiet, Giovanni Giacometti, Ferdinand Hodler, Sophie Taeuber-Arp and Félix Vallotton).

Ausstellung — Exhibition

Kuratoren — Curators
Iris Hutegger, Christoph Vögele

Assistenz — Assistant
Patricia Bieder

Sekretariat — Administration
Christine Kobel

Ausstellungsaufbau — Exhibition setup
Til Frentzel
Jürg Dreier
Daniel Lopez

Katalog — Catalog

Texte — Texts
Karine Tissot
Christoph Vögele

Übersetzungen — Translations
Text Karine Tissot: John O'Toole, New York
(Französisch/Englisch — French/English)
Text Christoph Vögele: Steve Gander, Wien
(Deutsch/Englisch — German/English)

Lektorat und Korrektorat — Proof-reading
Martina Buder, Dresden
Véronique Chevallier, Paris
Andrea Stettler, Ineuil

Gestaltung und Satz — Graphic Design and Typesetting
Guido Widmer, Zürich

Reprofotografie — Reprophotography
Serge Hasenböhler, Basel

Lithografie, Druck, Bindung — Lithography, Printing, Binding
DZA Druckerei zu Altenburg GmbH, Altenburg

© 2016 Kunstmuseum Solothurn, Verlag für moderne Kunst, Autorin und Autor
www.kunstmuseum-so.ch
www.vfmk.org

© 2016 Iris Hutegger, ProLitteris, Zürich
www.irishutegger.ch

Alle Rechte vorbehalten — All rights reserved
Printed in Germany

Erschienen im — Published by
VfmK Verlag für moderne Kunst GmbH
Salmgasse 4a
A-1030 Wien
hello@vfmk.org
www.vfmk.org

Vertrieb — Distribution
DE, AT und Europa — and Europe: LKG, www.lkg-va.de
CH: AVA, www.ava.ch
UK: Cornerhouse Publications, www.cornerhousepublication.org
USA: D.A.P., www.artbook.com

Bibliografische Information der Deutschen Nationalbibliothek
Die Deutsche Nationalbibliothek verzeichnet diese Publikation in der Deutschen Nationalbibliografie; detaillierte bibliografische Daten sind im Internet über http://dnb.dnb.de abrufbar.

Bibliographic information published by the Deutsche Nationalbibliothek
The Deutsche Nationalbibliothek lists this publication in the Deutsche Nationalbibliografie; detailed bibliographic data are available on the Internet at http://dnb.dnb.de

ISBN 978-3-903131-33-0

Diese Publikation erscheint anlässlich der Ausstellung
This publication accompanies the exhibition

Iris Hutegger und Alice Bailly

Kunstmuseum Solothurn
Graphisches Kabinett

20. August bis 30. Oktober 2016

Galerie Jacques Cerami, Charleroi

M&R
MARTINI & RONCETTI

Galleria Martini & Ronchetti, Genua

GalerieEstherWoerdehoff
Paris

prohelvetia